THE SPIRIT

Carthusian Reflections

A CARTHUSIAN

Photographs by
A Friend of the Community
of St Hugh's, Parkminster

DARTON·LONGMAN+TODD

First published in 1998 by
Darton, Longman and Todd Ltd
1 Spencer Court
140–142 Wandsworth High Street
London SW18 4JJ

ISBN 0–232–52295–2

Designed by Sandie Boccacci
Phototypeset in 10½/13 pt Aldus by Intype London Ltd
Printed and bound in Great Britain by
Halstan & Co Ltd, Amersham, Bucks

Contents

Introduction

Culture is embodied in artefacts that express meaning and capture something of the beauty of creation as perceived by the human mind. Matter and spirit have mysterious affinities and can mirror one another. This is seen in a particular way in the ensemble of buildings that constitute a monastery. The buildings are conceived in function of a spiritual ideal. They provide the setting in which a group of people can live the gospel message of Christ in a radical way according to a tradition handed down from the first centuries of Christendom. They are functional at two levels: as containing all that is necessary for a group of people at a material level – workshops, kitchen, community buildings – and at a spiritual level – a quiet retired location, church, chapter-house, hermitages, a certain aesthetic of construction that raises the mind towards spiritual things.

The overall form is of a number of hermitages (35) linked together by a cloister leading to a cluster of community buildings, at the centre of which is the church. A Charterhouse is a community of hermits. It is a reservoir of silence and peace, a conduit of prayer. Monks have lived, worked and prayed here since 1873. In some way, their spirit still inhabits the place. The sensitive eye discerns the fugitive traces they have left. The intuition of this fact by a Friend of the Community is at the origin of this book. He has tried to capture in his photographs the spirit embodied in the buildings, the tools, the light and forms of the monastery space.

The sermons that accompany these photographic studies are the very articulation of the events and liturgical celebrations that scan the life of the monastic community. They have no pretension whatever; delivered to the community alone in the chapter-house, they do express in words the same vision of reality and life as that contained in the photos. Like the Gregorian chant that fills the silence with the harmony of its sound they express a life of simple and robust faith imbued by the presence of God. The hope is that this book may communicate something of its peace and joy to all who look at it and read it.

LIGHT IN THE DARKNESS

Feast of the Presentation of the Lord, 2 February 1991

The next time you come into the Prior's office, look at the mantlepiece and you will see two reproductions of pictures by Rembrandt. One is of the father receiving into his embrace the prodigal son. The other is of Simeon receiving into his arms the child Christ. For many years now these two images have presided over my office of novice-master.

They express two truths absolutely fundamental for me, which I find again in today's feast. The first is precisely that the light that Christ came to reveal in his person and in his life is the immense love of the Father, totally gratuitous, forgiving and healing and so dramatically portrayed in the figure of the father of the prodigal son. Christ came to tell us who God is and how he is; to tell us what his name is, that it is 'Father'; and how much he loves us, so much that he gives us his only begotten Son.

This is the light which Christ is, and which illuminates our existence. Before this light the darkness of evil and war and sin will not prevail. Even death is defeated, for God's love is eternal and, desiring communion with us, makes us enter into his eternal life, beyond death. This is our belief, this is our hope, the light that guides our steps. It is not a light that is outside of us, but rather is it a light in our hearts that would transform our whole being. Born of God, we are called to walk as children of light. We are called to love as the Father loves in Christ.

The lighted candles which we will carry at tomorrow's celebration symbolise at once Christ himself, our faith and the Spirit of love which we bear in our hearts, the eternal spark of life that has been given to us as a promise and a task. 'Within your temple, Lord, we ponder your loving kindness,' sings the liturgy. Note that contemplation passes from a hearing of God's word to a certain seeing, which grasps more directly God's love. 'We have heard what God has done and now we have seen it, in the city of our God, on his holy mountain' (Response of the Mass). Our response is, as the alleluia has it: 'I will worship at your holy Temple and give thanks to your name.' The temple for us is not a material building, either in Jerusalem, Rome or here, but the temple that we have become by the inhabitation of the Spirit in our hearts.

In that inner temple, we may in all places and at all times praise and worship God (John 4:23–4). Our hearts may be a living altar from which constantly ascends before God pure prayer, with which all our acts should be imbued (statutes 4. 11). It is to this end that as the child Jesus was consecrated to God, so too we would consecrate our whole being to the Father in thanksgiving and in joy, asking the Mother of God to present us to him, as she once did her child.

That consecration is an ordering of our being and of all our powers to God's glory and love. But because we are ordered to something above ourselves there is an element of obscurity. Our faith penetrates into a domain where our intelligence cannot wholly follow. This is precisely the risk and the grandeur of faith which is, as the letter to the Hebrews put it (11:1 RSV), 'the assurance of things hoped for, the conviction of things not seen'.

This distance between our human condition and the spiritual reality of God is both ontological and moral. To see God, the heart must be pure, must then be purified, for we are all sinful human beings. This is evoked in the reading from Malachi where the presence of God is described as a coming of the Lord that shakes the heart to its foundations, and refines and purifies it. Only then can be made the offering to the Lord, as it should be made. God to us is also a consuming fire.

I find this beautifully portrayed in Rembrandt's painting of Simeon receiving the child into his arms. Very personally, I see here also the novice-master in his role of spiritual paternity: he too receives into his hands a young and hidden Christ. Now Rembrandt paints the old Simeon as physically blind. If you remember, the promise he had received was that he should not see death before he had *seen* the Lord's Christ. And living a righteous and devout life, he had believed and waited and hoped. Even now, an old blind man in whom the light of physical sight has died, he comes still to the temple, he believes still in God's promise, still he hopes. As Paul would say 'he hoped against hope' (Romans 4:18).

And now, one day, we see him, in hushed wonder, receive into his hands a wrapped up child whom, in the Spirit, he recognises as the one sent by God for the salvation of all. He sees finally, not with human eyes, for they have failed him, but with the eyes of the Spirit, the eyes of faith. And his old man's voice rings out in that vibrant hymn of praise that has echoed through the centuries, the 'Nunc dimittis':

'Now, Lord, you have kept your promise,
and you may let your servant go in peace.
With my own eyes I have seen your salvation,
which you have prepared in the presence of all peoples:
A light to reveal your will to the Gentiles,
and bring glory to your people Israel.'

Luke 2:29–32 GNB

I will finish by drawing your attention to a beautiful thought contained in the prayer for the blessing of the candles. Listen to it well. It says that each one of us who bear the light of Christ will be really a source of light in the measure of our joy. That joy, joy of Christ, I wish you on this day.

THE RETURN

First Sunday of Lent, 1991

On this entry into Lent, I would like simply to dwell for a moment on a few images that the liturgy puts before us these days. The older ones will remember that there was formerly no special mass for this Saturday. When it was decided in the 1970s to fill this gap, texts were chosen that gave the sense of the whole Lenten period. The mass could be used all through Lent as a votive mass in private, and can still be.

The introit announces already the meaning of the purification we aim at, names its author, for it is God himself who cleanses our hearts, and its end, a new spirit within us, a new creation in Christ:

> I will prove my holiness through you.
> I will gather you from the ends of the earth;
> I will pour clean water on you
> and wash away all your sins.
> I will give you a new spirit within you, says the Lord.
>
> *(Ezekiel 36:23–6)*

I like to see us as called by God from so many different countries to be purified in pardon and to render praise and glory to God. 'Merciful Father, [we pray] purify our hearts and make us fully your children by grace, so that we may look forward with joy to the paschal mysteries.' We have indeed need to be purified. Our hearts are heavy and selfish, we are slaves of many superficial appetites that our modern consumer world teaches us to deem necessities, though they are not: often they are but capricious children. To become truly free, to tend in truth towards the spiritual realities that draw us, we need to disengage our hearts and our minds from a multiplicity of secondary things. Then in all simplicity, we can adhere to that which is eternal and essential.

St Paul gives us a vigorous image of this: the runner fully stretched towards the finishing line, intent on this alone: God's prize to him who strives, life on high in Christ Jesus. Grasped by Christ Jesus, Paul frees himself from the multiple ties that bind him to his past, a slavery often deeper that that of our appetites. He gives no thought to what lies behind but pushes on to what is ahead. 'To know Christ and the power flowing

[5]

from his resurrection.' But how? There is only one way: 'sharing in his sufferings by being formed into the pattern of his death'. Thus he hopes to arrive at the resurrection from the dead, at the triumph of life and of love (Philippians 3:8–14 NAB).

This is what Lent is all about. But if it is an ardent thrust out of our petty selves towards God, it is also paradoxically an entering into the deeper self, the real heart's depths. To meet God, the gospel invites us to no exterior show but rather to enter into the secret place of our heart, where the Father alone awaits us. ' "Go into your room and shut the door and pray to your Father who is in secret; and your Father who sees in secret will reward you" ' (Matthew 6:6 RSV).

This is not the hiding from the gaze of others of the hypocrite, but the opening of the depths of the heart in total transparence to the Father, in confidence and love. Directly, simply, before him we are what we are. We offer what we are, with all our sins, and desires, and wounds, humbly and trustingly to the healing power of his grace. His light may at first hurt our weak eyes but soon it cures and gives life. The seeds of hate and violence and division which we see so terribly projected in large on the political stage these tragic times, the seeds in the heart of each one of us, are consumed and changed into seeds of love and peace, for ourselves and for all people. Such is the work that the Father effects in secret, little by little, if we persevere in his presence. This is the most valuable contribution we can make to our troubled times.

In time, as our knowledge/love of the Father grows, we will know ourselves to be enveloped in his knowledge/love of us. Our prayer will not have need of many words. Our hearts will often rest in silence. We will be content with the prayer Christ taught us to say: 'Father, hallowed be your name, your kingdom come'. *Your* name, *your* kingdom.

I would like to leave you another image of the Father towards whom we journey this Lenten time, an image which will perhaps complement that of Paul. It is that of the father who rushes forth to meet the prodigal son and embraces him. Again I invite you to meditate on the beautiful picture of Rembrandt. The son, and we are all his sons, sought his happiness in taking all he could get and in satisfying his selfish desires. It was only when he was reduced to destitution that he remembered his father's house. It is perhaps one reason for our Lenten privations. By voluntarily embracing a certain poverty we may accede to the memory of a deeper place of joy. All desire bears the trace of memory. Our going forward is also a going back to the source of all, to become what we are eternally in God. Remark the tenderness of the Father's welcome, the maternal gesture by which he clasps his son (note the worn sandals on his feet), clasps him to his bosom and to his heart. May this Lent be, for each of you, a journey back to the Father's love, the source of all life and joy, with Christ as guide, in his footsteps, through death to life, in the joy of the Holy Spirit.

A GRACE OF PASS-OVER

Easter Sunday, 1991

The Father has been the light we have followed these last months. The Father of our Lord Jesus Christ, who reveals to us the visage of his great love. I gave you the image of the prodigal son returning to the embrace of his father, as an image of the path of return to God which is the task of our Lenten conversion.

It seems to me that the Paschal mystery of Christ's death and resurrection can be understood in this way. There also we see the Son passing from a condition of extreme poverty and dereliction into the eternal embrace of the Father's love. Christ himself was no sinner, but he had so accepted solidarity with us in our fallen state that we also, with all that we are of sin and mediocrity, penetrate with him into the kingdom of the resurrection.

The passion of Christ manifests in the most cruel way the reality of evil and violence and death in human history, and in the heart of each one of us. For history, yesterday's or today's, is only what is in our own heart, thrown onto the larger public screen. But God does not abandon human beings to their violence and death, nor reject them. He is no philosopher's abstraction in some untouchable ethereal sphere: he is the Father of humanity. In Christ, he takes his place at our side and carries the burden of our sin on the cross for love of humankind. It is this love (which is Love) that triumphs over the powers of evil and death, and resuscitates Christ and us with him.

We have truly passed with Christ into the world of the resurrection in the measure that we are led by this Love, which is given to each one of us in the gift of the Holy Spirit. The resurrection is not something in the past, circumscribed in time and place. It is the supreme act of God in history. In so far as it is the act of God it transcends time and place and is as present and active today as on the first Easter morning. In a particular way, the celebration of the Eucharist renders it close to us in sign and symbol, permitting our lives of each day and our hearts to be caught up in the movement of return to the Father and of love of others in Christ.

We know now that he whom we call God is indeed the Father, the source and end of all being, and that he is with us always in the risen Christ. With us in all our humanity and weakness. Christ has sought us out in every possible depth of our being, to bring us light and love and healing. And he still does. The fact of the resurrection assures us that his spirit will never be vanquished by sin or death in our hearts and in the world. We are, we exist, by the gift of God's love, we are redeemed by the power of that same love. If we open our hearts to it, it will be a force of love and joy within us.

This does not mean that we are instantly propelled into some celestial sphere, where all is perfect. As with Jesus, the grace of God is a grace of pass-over, a grace that enables us to live our human life and death in faith. To combat the evil in us and around us, so as to sow the seeds of justice and of love. To believe and to persevere through the dark places of weakness, frustration, despair, illness, obscurity of mind, and finally death. For we know that here, particularly here, God in Christ is with us, near to us, in us, sharing our burden, as we too can share his in others (Colossians 1:24), if I may so express myself. The grace of the resurrection in us takes the form of hope in faith, for ourselves and for all people, however desperate may seem their case. It is not a magic wand that banishes the evils of the world, but rather a mysterious force that is capable of transforming everything, even death, in love and life. The wounds remain in Christ's risen body but they are transfigured. God's ways are mysterious for our little minds. His strength is made perfect in weakness. His Spirit builds unerringly a new and more wonderful creation with the unlikely material that we are.

This same grace of resurrection is at work in our community as such, here and now. This we cannot doubt. But how do we discern it, what form does it take? I wonder how we should see the grace of the resurrection at work in our community at this present time.

Should we ask of God and expect that everything will suddenly go well, that healths will not fail, that a lot of novices should enter and stay, that there will be no tensions or misunderstandings between persons, that the financial problems should all disappear? Perhaps that is what will happen, perhaps not. And if it were not so to come about, by what criteria do we judge that this is failure or success? The final criterion, is it not, is that it is God's work, the realisation of *his* will, and this alone. To see things in this way, we must place ourselves at a deeper level of faith. It is a paschal mystery that is being realised in our community, as in each individual. That we are, in some respects, poor, vulnerable and imperfect is no obstacle to God's work being done. He prefers to work with what is, in itself, nothing. He declares that it is the poor in spirit who is blessed. To be poor in spirit means accepting to be detached from the trappings of exterior success or riches, and letting go of our own reasonable project and wisdom and interest so that the mysterious plan of God's love and wisdom may bear its fruit. We must cling to nothing for its or our own sake. We must, I think, abandon in joyful hope our community, our house and its future into the hands of the Father, knowing that in Christ he is closer than ever to us in our poverty and humility, and that no force in heaven or on earth can prevail against his Spirit. We shall, of course, do all we can do, for the Lord expects that of us (the angel rebuked the disciples who just stood there looking up at the clouds into which Christ disappeared in his ascension!), but with liberty and peace of mind, knowing that what the Spirit is bringing to being is a spiritual kingdom, an interior reality of the order of the heart, a new creation in the mysterious image of Christ to the glory of the Father.

I would like to finish by wishing you that peace that our Lord invoked on his disciples after his resurrection: 'Peace be with you.'

THEN IT HAPPENS

Pentecost Sunday, 1991

I did not choose it, but it seems that my priorate is beginning under the patronage of the Holy Spirit. I could not ask better, of course, and yet . . . The Spirit, or rather, the effects of his action, are often disturbing of the status quo, and sometimes, to human eyes, ambiguous. There is a constant dialectic between tradition, that which is established, venerated and handed on, and the breath of the Spirit, giving newness of life and seeking new forms of creative expression. So it has always been in the Church, and it is a condition of life and development. A living organism, while maintaining its essential identity, must yet adapt to its environment or die. This operation, for those involved, may be a source of deep anxiety as it touches the external supports of people's sense of security. Very often they will react aggressively, in a passive or active way. All this is normal if not comfortable. Let us see if the feast we are celebrating can cast some light on the matter.

The disciples were not particularly outstanding on the human level. Even after the resurrection of Christ and his appearing to them, they still seem to be a frightened group of disorientated people. It is as if the paschal victory of Christ remains outside them. They believe, but they are not transformed. They pray together but their prayer, like their faith, is bounded by their fears. They are prisoners of what they have known, of their religious ideas and forms.

Then it happens. Their prayer at last succeeds in opening their fearful hearts to the outpouring of the Spirit. Those hearts are truly changed. They are now full of courage and joy. They receive the power to bear witness in their words and in their lives to the life of the Spirit-gift. Little by little they will discover the radical liberty of Christ's Spirit within them and the forms his love will forge for itself in the Church. They will meet with resistance and persecution, but the life of which they are bearers will not be denied.

That same principle of new life is within our hearts too, perhaps like smouldering embers. It awaits the stirring of our faith and hope for the Spirit to breathe upon the embers and bring them to flame. This is what we ask when we invoke the Spirit. 'Come, Holy Spirit, fill our hearts and kindle within them the fire of your love.' As in Ezekiel's dream, we would that the Spirit breathe upon our dry bones and bring them to life. Let us then be present, listening to his often quiet murmur, receptive to his every movement.

We must learn to distinguish his action from all the other impulses, more or less egocentric and obscure, that traverse us. In these last weeks, at the level of the community, two clear signs have been given, objective ecclesial signs, far surer than subjective ones. Firstly, the decision of the Definitory at the General Chapter as to the further orientation of the house and its foundation, and the implicit confidence put in our noviciate. Secondly, the vote of the community electing its prior. Over and beyond the subjective reasons, always more or less imperfect and more or less well-informed, that motivated the individual persons, we can see and acquiesce to the Holy Spirit who realises the design of God in his Church, in particular the living organism of the Church that we form together here in St Hugh's. Whatever our personal preferences, we can all unite together in the implementation of what now appears clearly as God's will for us.

We will be able to recognise the work of the Spirit by its fruits: 'love, joy, peace, patience, kindness, goodness, faithfulness, humility and self-control' (Galatians 5:22 GNB) Love, of course, is the first and primary fruit of the Spirit, for the Spirit is the bond of love between the Father and the Son, and by way of consequence, between us too. That bond creates communion and unity.

Let us ask particularly for the grace of the unity that is the work of the Spirit. A unity based on a deep faith and expressing itself in mutual respect and acceptance of others, albeit in their difference. This house has been plagued by a certain lack of unity for many years. Our task is to create that unity in Christ, otherwise the house will surely fall.

As a model of what we must strive towards, I will end by a rather long citation from Paul's letter to the Ephesians (4:1–7, 11b–13, 16b GNB):

> I urge you then – I who am a prisoner because I serve the Lord: live a life that measures up to the standard God set when he called you. Be always humble, gentle and patient. Show your love by being tolerant with one another. Do your best to preserve the unity which the Spirit gives by means of the peace that binds you together.

There is one body and one spirit, just as there is one hope to which God has called you. There is one Lord, one faith, one baptism; there is one God and Father of all mankind, who is Lord of all, works through all, and is in all.

Each one of us has received a special gift in proportion to what Christ has given . . . He appointed some to be apostles, others to be prophets, others to be evangelists, others to be pastors and teachers. He did this to prepare all God's people for the work of Christian service, in order to build up the body of Christ. And so we shall all come together to that oneness in our faith and in our knowledge of the Son of God: we shall become mature people, reaching to the very height of Christ's full stature . . . when each separate part (of the body) works as it should, the whole body grows and builds itself up through love.

Come, O Holy Spirit, fill our hearts – hearts of flesh created in us by you – and kindle within them the fire of your love. May it be so for each one of us and for all together, this Pentecost, which will mark, I pray and hope, a new beginning for us all.

HEAVEN BOUND

Receiving the Habit as Cloister Monk,
Feast of the Assumption of the Blessed Virgin Mary,
15 August 1991

Christopher-Mary, you have chosen to receive the Carthusian habit on the feast of the Assumption of Our Lady into heaven. The feast designates the end towards which you must tend, the name, the way that you must follow to get there.

The feast of the Assumption of Our Lady celebrates the full realisation of our hope. In it, the Church affirms her faith that Mary has entered with her full human being, body and soul, into the world of God, the kingdom of God, the world of the resurrection. In her, the divine reality that is present in a hidden way in us by grace has achieved its plenitude.

So we celebrate Our Lady's joy, the eternal joy and love that has been so splendidly given her. She is the first fruit of Christ's grace. The Church sees in her that which she is called to become.

The image that first comes to mind is, of course, the image of an ascension, a going up into a higher sphere. The book of Revelation, in the reading for the Mass of the feast (21:1–5a NAB), to illustrate that this is the work of God's grace alone, speaks of a descent, God coming to and being with us.

> I saw a new Jerusalem, the holy city,
> coming down out of heaven from God,
> beautiful as a bride prepared to meet her husband.
> I heard a loud voice from the throne cry out:
> This is God's dwelling among men.

The two images complete one another. Their use in the liturgy, the sort of passing back and forth of the regard between Mary and the Church, underlines the fact that Our Lady is seen as the icon of the Church and therefore as a model for each one of us.

We too are called to enter, body and soul, into the full union with God. Your taking of the habit today symbolises a deep commitment to orientate all your forces and desire towards the kingdom of heaven.

With Guigo you are saying by your act that nothing should be clung to but what is eternal.

With St Paul, pressed by the love of Christ, you would in your turn press on, 'forgetting what lies behind and straining forward to what lies head. I [you say] press on towards the goal for the prize of the upward call of God in Christ Jesus' (Philippians 3:14 RSV). You must have something of the urgency, the passion of a man who has glimpsed a reflection of the incomprehensible love of God in Christ Jesus and would tend with his whole heart towards it.

Our real home, our real country is not the earthly one with its dissensions, its ephemeral avidities, its deaths. Our country 'is in heaven, and from it we await a Saviour, the Lord Jesus Christ, who will change our lowly body to be like his glorious body, by the power which enables him even to subject all things to himself' (Philippians 3:20 RSV).

Then you will be clothed not only with a white habit but with that which the habit signifies, Christ himself. Christopher means the bearer of Christ. You must become what you are called, you must be transformed into Christ. And the habit recalls that this means living, or letting Christ live in you, his paschal mystery: 'That [you] may know him [Christ Jesus] and the power of his resurrection, and may share his sufferings, becoming like him in his death, that if possible [you] may attain the resurrection from the dead' (Philippians 3:10–11 RSV).

You are called to live this sublime reality, not as something esoteric, far away, but as the substance of your everyday life. There the example of Mary is precious. She is the translation into simple, transparent everyday living and acts of that adhesion to God's loving will which is the essence of faith. That is what the monastic life in its materiality is all about. So that all things may be made new.

Let me finish with an exhortation again from Paul. May it inspire your monastic life and fire your faith and your love.

> If then you have been raised with Christ, seek the things that are above, where Christ is, seated at the right hand of God [and Our Lady with him]. Set your minds on things that are above, not on things that are on earth. For you have died and your life is hid with Christ in God. When Christ who is our life appears, then you also will appear with him in glory. (Colossians 3:1–3 RSV)

THE NEW EVE

Feast of the Birthday of the Blessed Virgin Mary,
8 September 1991

To celebrate someone's birthday is to celebrate the fact that they exist as persons, that they have received the gift of life. God's creative word has called them from nothingness into conscious being, and we are glad. We share the joy of that being and we give thanks.

This is seen very clearly in the way the liturgy celebrates Our Lady's birthday. It is pure celebration. A cascade of poetical images evokes the blossoming of this flower of unique beauty on the old tree of humanity, whose trunk and branches the genealogy of St Matthew's Gospel evokes summarily. A pure note rings out of the cacophony of history's sound. God's melody is sung. You remember how the first response of Matins puts it:

> I see her, beautiful as a dove, coming up the river's bank.
> A priceless perfume embalms her garments.
> Like a summer's day, roses surround her, and lilies of the valley.

I am reminded of Botticelli's painting of Venus advancing on the waves of the sea in the first dawn of her creation. The connection is not fortuitous, for Mary is the new Eve who will give birth to the new Adam and thus render possible the new creation. God's work shines forth in its pristine purity: beyond sin. This is how God's creation should be.

I like to think of Our Lady as a deeply joyful person, receiving the gift of life at each moment with wonder and gratitude, conscious of the enormous gift life is. And this in a simple, direct way, translucent to the love of God expressed in all things, including her own being and vitality. For God is above all the living God and it is through the experience of life that we begin to glimpse something of his being. Humankind alone of earth's creatures is conscious of the gift of life. We alone can give thanks for it and praise and adore the Giver. How full the psalms are of this praise and adoration and how they give voice to the whole of creation. The sun, the stars, the seas, the mountains, birds, animals, all God's creatures, through the mouth of human beings praise this Lord, the Giver and sustainer of life.

It is given to humankind also to explore all the dimensions of life. Conscious of the fragile, sacred thing it is, death casts its shadow on human joy. Are we but the flower of a day, God's plaything but not his kin? What is the ultimate sense of our life, our final destination? Our spirit desires a plenitude of life beyond earthly limits, a conscious communion with Being. Is this illusory, doomed to frustration?

No, it is not. From the beginning we are made for God. We are made in his image so as to be able to participate in his life. We are radically capable of knowing and loving God as he is in himself, of becoming part of the prodigious exchange of love and light that constitutes the life of the Holy Trinity. This is life's secret, its pure flame, and in its incandescent purity, it is without diminution or end. This is eternal life, to know (meaning both know and love, at once, in the Hebrew sense of the word) God the Father, the source of all life, and Jesus Christ, the splendour of his brightness, his Son, in the Spirit of their love, which is the ultimate gift of his passion to us, making us children of God, heirs of Christ.

Our Lady's birthday is there as the dawn of a day that will see God. Her total openness to God will be the place of God's coming to us. The flower, albeit a passion flower, will be Christ. She will be a mother, one who communicates life. He will *be* the Way, the Light and the Life. And of his fullness we have all received. With Mary, let us celebrate joyfully and simply the gift of God, the life that ultimately is God himself.

THE STANDARD OF HOLINESS

Feast of All Saints, 1 November 1991

The celebration of the feast of all those who have attained the goal of their lives invites us to reflect on the fact that each one of us is called to personal sanctity. It is not enough to get through life somehow, to avoid doing too much evil and meriting punishment – we are called to be saints.

This is the standard by which we should judge our acts and our lives, the standard of holiness. This may seem pretentious and yet there it is. 'Be perfect as the Father is perfect'; 'Be holy, as I am holy' says Our Lord. And what is religious life but a conscious striving towards this holiness? It is too easy to forget it; to become so caught up in the pursuit of other legitimate but inferior things that we forget the essential. Our needs and thirsts, our self-affirmation, our vanity, our satisfaction, even spiritual – all these things become the effective springs of our actions. They are perhaps not wrong in their place, but often they are centred on our small grasping ego. We must constantly ask: 'Where is the sanctity in all that?' This is the equivalent of saying 'Where is God in all that?' For this is sanctity, to be God-centred, to live in and for God. And it is the equivalent of asking 'Where is the love in all that?' For God is love. He who abides in love abides in God and God in him. This is the holiness to which we are called.

It would indeed be pretentious to aspire to sanctity, if God had not given us a thirst for it, in giving us the gift of his Spirit. The Spirit is the gift of God's own love, the gift of his own holiness. Holiness for us, then, is letting this Spirit of Love inspire all our actions and our being, making us children of the Father. Far from being a Herculean affirmation of self, it is the emptying of self so that Christ may come to be in us.

To save your life you must lose it, to receive all you must let go of all. Where then will we look for the saints? Amongst the rich, the powerful, the fully satisfied, the gifted? There may be saints among them if a deeper level of openness exists in their hearts, but it is harder for them. Christ in the gospel invites us to look for the saints among the poor in heart, the humble, the meek, the makers of peace, the persecuted for his sake. He gives himself as an example to follow, he who is meek and humble of heart, he who gives his life for love of his brothers and sisters, who does always the will of his Father and walks constantly in his presence and in his love. Let us look in our hearts. St Paul tells us bluntly, whatever else is there, knowledge, sacrifice, generosity, apparent virtue, if there is not love, we are nothing in terms of holiness. If we can accept even this great poverty and turn to God in faith, asking him to give us this gift of love that is beyond our powers, it can become the poverty of heart that is called blessed by Our Lord.

The way of the desert is perhaps a way of especial poverty, or rather of an acute awareness of this essential poverty in love and in holiness. But from this place of poverty of self, the monk believes in the gift of God and holds firm in the hope of the realisation of God's promise. To such is promised the kingdom of heaven.

Let us celebrate, then, the happiness of our brothers and sisters who have entered into the joy of the Lord, and keep our eyes fixed on the goal as we follow Christ, in the Spirit, towards the Father.

IN HIS TEMPLE

Feast of the Presentation of the Lord, 2 February 1992

'Suddenly there will come to the temple the Lord whom you seek.'
(Malachi 3:2 NAB)

We spend many hours each day and night in a building we call a church (from Greek *Kyriakon*, the [house] of the *Kyrios*, Lord). I would like to reflect briefly with you on the significance of this fact.

At all times, and in all religions, people have tended to create holy spaces, places with which the divine presence was deemed to be associated in some way. In the more developed religions at least, where the existence of a universal God was recognised, this did not imply that God was crudely localised, circumscribed in a particular place. Rather it symbolised the divine presence and helped the believer to enter into contact with it.

We find this also in the Old Testament. The God of the desert period refused any fixed abode other than the tent of meeting. His was a dynamic presence, marching at the head of his people, represented by a pillar of fire by night and a pillar of cloud by day. When the people settled in Palestine, God's presence as it were settled too, in the temple in Jerusalem. There, he assured Solomon the builder, he would hear those who called to him and receive their worship. 'I have consecrated this house which you have built, and put my name there for ever; my eyes and my heart will be there for all time' (1 Kings 9:3 RSV). Yet Solomon is well aware of God's freedom, even with regard to the temple. 'Will God indeed dwell on earth? Behold, heaven and the highest heaven cannot contain thee; how much less this house which I have built!' (1 Kings 8:27 RSV). God is present in all his creation. He will not, cannot be enchained by human beings.

Furthermore, God's presence in the temple of Jerusalem is conditional upon the people faithfully doing his will and keeping his commandments (9:4). But, with time, hearts grow cold and the temple is perverted from its original purpose. It is no longer a house of prayer, but a place of commercial exploitation by the priests. The prophets fight to purify it time and time again, but they never wholly succeed. The tendency to put confidence in the material and visible seems uncontrollable,

making even God's house a means of security and self-glorification. There is a constant tension between the purity of the perception of God's nature, expressed in the inner sanctuary where no image of God was permitted, and the materiality of the temple worship, necessary though it be. The movement is too often trapped in the symbol and refracted; it does not pass through to God himself in true worship.

Something radical is necessary and Christ brings it. He submits to the temple ritual and teaches and walks there as one known to his people. It is his Father's house. Yet he shows a rare violence with regard to it. He chases the money-lenders. He weeps over the obduracy of its people. He predicts its destruction. A time will come when the Father will not be worshipped exclusively in this or that place, however venerable, but 'in spirit and in truth'. God is spirit and what he wants is the worship of the human spirit, the homage of our mind and heart. How? Where?

Christ makes this extraordinary statement: 'Destroy this temple (of Jerusalem) and I will build it up in three days.' Those who heard did not, could not understand. But we do. 'He spoke of the temple of his body' (John 2:21 RSV), the new life and worship that his death and resurrection would make possible by the gift of the Holy Spirit to his body, the Church. This now is the true temple, the place of God's dwelling. Each one of us has received that Spirit of Christ by which we cry 'Abba, Father', the Spirit which prays in us with a prayer beyond our understanding. And as Christ was God incarnate, so too our bodies, not just our souls, become the temple of God, for God's Spirit dwells in them (1 Corinthians 3:16). This, for Paul, is the ultimate reason why we should respect our bodies, for in them, rather than in something outside ourselves, is realised that incarnation of the divine presence that the temple worship symbolised. The worship of the Spirit will be expressed in the acts of the body but the source is within, their whole value is in their weight of faith and love.

Our care should be to plunge ourselves constantly in the source of the Spirit within us. As our Statutes put it, 'Let our heart be a living altar from which there constantly ascends before God pure prayer, with which all our acts should be imbued' (4.11). This is the sense of our solitude. This will be our worship of the Father in truth, for Christ is our truth. 'In solitude let the monk's soul be like a tranquil lake, whose waters well up from the purest source of the spirit, and . . . like a clear mirror reflect one image only, that of Christ' (13.15).

Let us take advantage of today's feast to renew the consecration of ourselves to the Father with all our strength and mind and heart, in uniting it to that of Christ. We shall then become like the servants of God described in the Apocalypse:

> 'Who are these, clothed in white robes, and from whence have they come?' . . . 'These are they who have washed their robes and made them white in the blood of the Lamb. Therefore are they before the throne of God, and serve him day and night within his temple; and he who sits upon the throne will shelter them with his presence. They shall hunger no more, neither thirst any more; . . . For the Lamb in the midst of the throne will be their shepherd, and he will guide them to springs of living water.' (Revelation 7:13–17 (in part) RSV).

THE FAST THAT GOD WANTS

First Sunday of Lent, 1992

Lent is a time of fasting. We abstain from certain satisfactions of the appetites of the body in order to purify the passions and liberate the spirit. That this is not automatic is clearly enough stated by the ironic attack of Isaiah on the fasters of his time, that we read at Mass last Friday (Isaiah 58:1–9a NAB). 'Is this the manner of fasting I wish, says the Lord . . . that a man afflict himself, bow his head like a reed and lie in sackcloth and ashes', while at the same time indulging in injustice, 'quarreling and fighting?'

The exterior practice is not enough, it is even of no value whatsoever, if it is not accompanied by an interior fasting directed towards a purification of the inner heart. A fasting from what, then? From injustice towards our neighbour, from 'quarreling and fighting', from all the works of selfishness, pride, vanity, self-affirmation, aggressivity, in a word, from all the manifestations of non-love.

Or put more positively, the fasting God wants are the works of love of our neighbour: compassion, sharing, helping the needy in whatever way we can. How far this goes is indicated in the gospel of the same Friday. We must be 'perfect as our heavenly Father is perfect'. In what way? By loving our enemies and praying for those who persecute us (Matthew 5:43—6:4). By not loving only those who love us, but by loving those who do not love us. Therefore, not only the works of love, but love of the heart itself.

We want to, but can we? Some of the exterior works of love we can rise to, perhaps, but love itself, the movement of the heart? Is it always love that moves us, is it not often irritation, censoriousness, rivalry, plain dislike? And it is the heart that counts. It is out of the heart that come evil thoughts, attitudes and acts (Matthew 15:19). The fasting that God wants will seek to purify the heart. It will abstain from, not only the exterior acts, but also the inner thoughts of non-love. But how? This is delicate. It is not enough to repress these thoughts from our consciousness. This is a way of denying their existence, of not owning them and consequently of not healing and going beyond them.

No, these thoughts and impulses are ours, our hearts are not free

[25]

of the self-love and pride which makes everyone a potential enemy. Let us own the sin within us. We will gain in self-knowledge, in humility and in realisation of our need of God's pardon and of the gratuitousness of his love. Thank God for Christ!

There is a subtle perversion one sometimes meets nowadays, that of the person who not only acknowledges the passions within him, but who flaunts them openly as a sign of superiority over less strong characters who dare not show the evil undoubtedly present in their hearts also.

It is not enough then to own our passions, we must try to purify and transform them. It is no hypocrisy, not to make others suffer at the level of exterior acts, even if the tempest rages within; but we do want to calm the tempest, at least in time. There is a fasting from injurious acts, and there is a fasting from injurious thoughts, if we use the word in the sense the desert fathers gave it, i.e. the thought plus its emotional charge.

This fasting from thoughts may take the form of an interior vigilance over what thoughts we allow into our mind, rejecting thoughts of judgement, criticism, violence, and accepting those of understanding, patience, love. It is in our power, usually, to fix our attention on the good qualities of a person or a situation, and not on the less good. Our thoughts will then be thoughts of peace and our acts will follow. We can choose to counteract any movements of aggressivity towards others, by deliberately, in our minds, affirming the other who annoys us in what he is and can become in Christ. All this within our own heart. The acts will follow. This is a form of intimate self-denial, a fast that pleases God who is love. For all non-love flows from love of self.

One could think of this also as interior silence. It cannot be sustained though, unless it draws its force from that silence of God which is his infinite love and mercy. Everything in Christ and in God is yes: yes to all the beings the gift of his love sustains. Never no: you shall not be.

It is prayer, the opening of our hearts to the silent love of God within us, which will gradually purify the source of our thoughts and passions. Not that they disappear necessarily. Rather, prayer enables us to enter into the depths of our heart, near to the creative source of God's love. Rather like a person diving into the sea, plunging through the moving surface of waves open to every wind, then through the upper water where fishes of many sizes and colours – some dangerous – come and go (these are our thoughts and passions), and finally attaining a depth where all is calm. From this place of the deep heart, the swimmer can see the movement of the surface, the busy world of the upper water, but is not carried along by it, the peace of the depths is not disturbed. The words spoken from this silent place will be words of love. These are the alms in secret which the Father rewards.

The fast that God wants from us then is the abstaining from the thoughts and works which do not come from love, and the doing of those that flow from the source of love within our hearts, that we reach in prayer. Do this and Our Lord promises:

> Then your light shall break forth like the dawn,
>   and your wound shall quickly be healed . . .
> Then shall you call, the Lord will answer,
>   You shall cry for help, and he will say,
>   Here I am!
>
> *(Isaiah 58:8–9 NAB)*

YOU WILL BE A LONG TIME DEAD

Easter Sunday, 1992

I wrote this sermon on Holy Saturday, that strange day when the grain of wheat lies dormant in the earth, given up, it seems, to decay. Let us not jump too lightly over this sort of distance between the oblation of the cross and the glory of the resurrection. For, in a sense, this is our place as we wait in hope, with all the creation, for the redemption of our bodies (Romans 8). This is monastic time.

'Truly, truly, I say to you, unless a grain of wheat falls into the earth and dies, it remains alone; but if it dies, it bears much fruit' (John 12:24 RSV). Time, years, consecrated to God in principle by our profession or donation, yet not yet transfigured. Already redeemed in hope from the inexorable logic of linear time that goes towards extinction, our time has in it already something of eternity, a wholly other dimension; yet it is subject to the laws of matter and decay, and of project and failure, of ideal and fault. It remains human time, measured more by its spiritual emotional content than by the clock.

No two times are the same. Your time is not my time. The child's endless hours, the young man's absorbed and pregnant hours, the old man's fleeting time, slipping through his fingers like fine sand, all these are qualitatively different times.

The value of human time, its real value, can be seen only against the background of eternity. This is particularly true in adversity. As the Irish saying crustily has it, cutting through any temptation towards self-pity before life's ills: 'You will be a long time dead.' Or as St Paul more elegantly expresses it:

> I consider that the sufferings of this present time are not worth comparing with the glory about to be revealed to us . . . We know that the whole creation has been groaning in labour pains until now, and not only the creation, but we ourselves, who have the first fruits of the Spirit, groan inwardly while we wait for adoption, the redemption of our bodies. For in hope we were saved. (Romans 8: 18, 22–4 NRSV)

Our time is mortal time, measured out. We know this yet we cling to it. Instead of celebrating the entry into the time of the resurrection, the consummation of our journey, we regard every day, every year gained as a victory over our mortality. A person is congratulated for having endured longer than another, irrespective of the quality of life involved. All that proves is that the husk of the grain is more resistant. But the value of the grain is in the kernel, the principle of life and growth which must break open the husk if it is to live.

The other day a novice showed me a chestnut he had cleverly picked up. A shoot had forced its way out of the husk and pushed its way into the ground in search of nourishment. The husk would soon fall away and be discarded. Why then do we hang on to the husk? Is it fear? Fear of annihilation, of pain, of dying, of the unknown? These are the natural fears of the sensible person. Christ too knew fear. But is there not another fear, fear of judgement, for we are responsible, must answer for the use of our time? Temperaments differ. The sanguine will tend to be trustful and optimistic. The narcissistic need to justify their every deed, can admit to no wrong. The melancholic, in face of the extreme demands they make on themselves, can see no good in themselves, can do no right. I oversimplify, of course. Finally, our liberty, like God's grace, is a mystery. Better, wiser, never to judge. In fact, this space of uncertainty allows us to let in something of God's eternity, in his merciful pardon. We can open and always reopen the dimension of eternity in our own lives (for we must not judge ourselves) and in the lives of others by the virtue of our non-judging and our pardon, which is at once a space of hope given to the other. Thus we can exorcise fear in ourselves.

> 'Do not judge and you will not be judged; do not condemn and you will not be condemned. Forgive and you will be forgiven, give and it will be given to you. A good measure, pressed down, shaken together, running over, will be put into your lap; for the measure you give will be the measure you get back.' (Luke 6:37–8 NRSV)

Of God's gift in the risen Christ, this good measure, pressed down, running over, I wish you all this Easter Day.

YOUR OLD MEN SHALL DREAM DREAMS

Pentecost Sunday, 1992

'In the last days, says God, I shall pour out my Spirit
on all mankind; and your sons and daughters shall prophesy;
your young men shall see visions, and your old men shall
dream dreams.'

(Acts 2:17, quoting Joel 2:28 NAB)

Old men are naturally inclined to look rather towards the past, to relive
and rehash the days of their youth. The Spirit, however, would turn
their minds towards the future, a future defined by God's promises. He
would have them dream dreams. There are of course dreams and dreams.

Some dreams are the voice of the past, our own past and that of the
human race. Other dreams are intimations of the future; they cast a
divinatory light on what is to come. And there are dreams that project
what we desire, the state of things that we hope for. Some of these may
be, in the popular expression, pipe-dreams, sheer trips of the imagination,
which merely take the place of the real and its required effort and
commitment. But there are others, the real dreams, that are like a star
towards which we direct our energies, and these are rooted in real
possibilities. They give form to the creative vitality within us.

Such dreams may be awakened in us by the Spirit. They may be our
response to the promises of God, the surge of our being towards their
realisation. They are infinitely precious, perhaps the best of each one of
us. They are capable of mobilising our energies to realise them in
concrete fact, giving unity and purpose to our lives.

Time will take its toll, of course. The young man easily 'sees visions'.
The old man knows the force of gravity pulling us constantly back to
earth. His hope will be tried and his danger is to lose the courage
to dream dreams. It is perhaps also the tendency of many young men
today. They cannot believe strongly enough in values above them,
capable of drawing them beyond their small worlds. They prefer the
security of their narrow but known boundaries to the risk of the dream.

Let us profit from this celebration of the Holy Spirit to renew our
dream and our hope. If I may so express myself, the Holy Spirit *is*

our future. Let us plunge our hearts in him as in a source, and streams of living water will flow.

What is our dream? Can we give it concrete shape? Is that not what our whole way of life is about? The realisation in this world of time of God's kingdom visibly and tangibly, in a place and in a time; and, simultaneously, the realisation of the deepest capacity and desire of each of our human hearts. To live by and in the Spirit of Christ, and thus to be animated by the Spirit of God and participate in the divine life. And to become, many though we are (all humankind in principle), one in God. A oneness capable of receiving and being in fraternal communion with people of all races and languages; of being a house for the poor in heart, like the Father's house, with many and diverse rooms, each full of his praise.

Is this too much to dream, or is it not Christ's prayer and God's promise?

Monastic life has always looked back to the apostolic church as to the model of the society it wanted to create. Let us see how it is described in the Acts of the Apostles.

First there is the period of waiting. On leaving the disciples, Christ had declared that the gift promised by the Father would be given: they are to be baptised with the Holy Spirit. 'You will receive power when the Holy Spirit comes upon you and you will bear witness for me ... even to the farthest corner of the earth' (Acts 1:8 NAB, slightly adapted).

They prepare for this coming by being constantly at prayer, all together in one place with one accord, with Mary. 'Come, Holy Spirit,' they pray. And come he does: a strong driving wind, flames like tongues of fire resting on each one. They are filled with the Holy Spirit and begin to talk in other tongues as the Spirit gives them utterance. And each of the men of many nationalities who listen to them, hear them speaking in his own tongue 'the great things that God has done'. The first fruit of the Spirit is to break through the multiple barriers that separate people one from another, and render communication, and hence communion, possible, so that all can praise God together. This was their witness to the world in the power of the Spirit.

The same Spirit of unity makes disciples come together in a group for they are a people: they agree to hold everything in common. They sell their property and possessions and distribute to everyone according to his need. One and all they keep up their daily attendance at the temple, and breaking bread in their homes, they share their meals with unaffected joy as they pray to God and enjoy the favour of the whole people (see Acts 2, 44–7 NAB).

Not for long. The Christ they bear witness to is too revolutionary, too different from the world's ways; the Christians are soon persecuted. The Spirit becomes a force of courage and perseverance in the face of difficulties and suffering. This only welds them more closely together and does not diminish their joy. United in heart and soul, a small group swimming against the current of their time in every way, they are God's own work and bear, by their existence itself, powerful witness to the resurrection of the Lord Jesus.

It is not necessary to labour the point that the first monks, and those that followed them, saw themselves as the successors of the apostolic community. Their communities reproduced the same essential features of sharing, poverty, unity, prayer, joy and the witness of their lives in spite of a hostile environment.

May we too be animated by the same Spirit. May we open our hearts to his force and love, and bear witness by our lives before the world. Let us have the courage and the audacity of our faith; in the Spirit of Christ let us boldly dream our dreams.

FOR WONDER'S SAKE

Feast of the Birthday of St John the Baptist, 24 June 1992

> Through a chink too wide,
> There comes in
> no wonder.
>
> *(Patrick Kavanagh)*

I would like to leave you today with one simple idea, which may cast some light on the mentality of those who seek out a solitary life. On one level, there is restriction of life: information, social contact, exchange of ideas, affective relationships, variety of interests, all these are deliberately lessened. To what purpose? Surely this represents a diminution, if not a frustration, or a mutilation.

This would be the case if such a restriction were imposed as upon a prisoner, or a hostage. But our solitaries do it willingly, they seek a great simplicity of life. Why? For wonder's sake. Wonder is a sentiment of surprised admiration, of joyful awe, of celebration and communion, stemming from the perception of something of the beauty, the grandeur, the trace of God in his creation or in his works. It is a sentiment of gift: of being-as-given; a sentiment too of oneness and communion. And often it is the chink not too wide that lets in wonder. One tiny hidden flower and not the annual flower show with thousands of blossoms in pots. A simple blade of grass is enough if really seen with love and attention. One note of a bell on the evening air, one look from Christ, one word wholly true.

If the lens of a camera is too wide open, the light cannot focus in a clear image. The contemplative will sometimes narrow the lens of his attention in order to receive what gives itself to his eyes, and to be at one with him who gives himself to be seen in the manifold splendour of his creation. As children we were all capable of wonder. As adults, we must laboriously recapture something of the innocence of our first glimpse of the joy of being. To such is the kingdom of heaven revealed.

HEAR THE WORD OF GOD

Feast of the Assumption of the Blessed Virgin Mary,
15 August 1992

'Blessed are those who hear the word of God and keep it.'
(Luke 11:28 RSV, slightly adapted.)

Mary in her assumption into heaven is, of course, the icon of the hope of the Church, and of each one of us. We too hope, one day, to enter into the eternal beatitude of God. Today I would like to meditate a moment on the way to heaven. The gospel of the vigil puts it very succinctly: 'Blessed are those who hear the word of God and keep it.' Or, as another translation puts it (J. B. Phillips), who 'hear the word of God and obey it'.

Now, that does not sound too difficult, does it? To hear the word of God and obey it, and thus be blessed with God's blessing. Putting God's word into practice can, it is clear, often be difficult. We know what we should do, we want at least in some degree to do it, but we meet many obstacles in our hearts. There is often a lack of love and faith, and we are bound by many, often hidden, chains. So it is, and we must constantly walk in the consciousness of our frailty. This becomes, however, joyous humility before the discovered gracious love of God, and a new reason to love and praise him. This is the blessedness of the poor in spirit, who have Christ ever with them.

But the first part, the hearing of the word of God – surely this is straightforward? We are not deaf, are we, nor dense? We are Christians, we have received the gift of faith and the anointing of the Spirit, the Word of God is our patrimony. This is true, yet let us not be presumptuous. Christ's critics replied similarly to him when he promised liberty to those who would be faithful to his word. 'You will know the truth and the truth will set you free' (John 8:32 GNB). Those he addressed were insulted. Christ implied that they, the chosen people, were not free! They rejected his words, they would have killed him if they could. And Our Lord goes on to show them why they cannot hear or understand his words, which are, however, the truth that he has heard from God.

First, he says, you are not free, for everyone who commits sin is a slave and obeys the Evil One. Secondly such a one is deaf to Truth.

> 'Why do you not understand my words?' [says Christ] 'It is because you cannot bear to hear what I am really saying. Your father is the devil, . . . a liar and the father of lies. And it is because I speak the truth that you will not believe me . . . The man who is born of God can hear the words of God and the reason you cannot hear the words of God is simply this, that you are not the sons of God.' (John 8:43–4a, 45, 47 Phillips)

You cannot hear because you do not draw your life from God, you are not really his sons. This is a terrible saying. We can be so certain at times, without dreaming that the measure of what we can perceive is but our own emptiness, or fullness of ourselves, our vanity and self-love, our fears and desires. To God's word we can turn a deaf ear, and the tragedy is that we are not even aware of our deafness. God's thoughts are not our thoughts: we tend, however, to take our thoughts for God's thoughts.

At this point, while I was writing this sermon, Dom Aloysius came in to tell me the result of the hearing-test he had taken in Horsham. He was advised to obtain a hearing-aid which will amplify the sound and, hopefully, help him to hear better. I could not help wondering what form a spiritual hearing-aid would take. Paradoxically, its function would not be to amplify the sounds coming in from the exterior, but rather to mute them, to distance us from them, while amplifying the wavelength of faith, and rendering us more sensitive to the inner voice of the Spirit, making itself heard in the deep place of the heart.

To hear God's thoughts, we need to quieten the tumult of our own thoughts and desires. God's word is heard in the silence of our hearts, in the humility of our minds, when we have turned away from our own interests and passions, towards his glory and his light. It is only then that the Spirit can give us to hear with God's ears, as it were, the eternal newness of his thought for us, to experience the reality of his love for us.

This is the serene silence with which Mary welcomed the Spirit in her 'Fiat'. Her assumption into heaven is the entry into the plenitude of that silence in which all things are uttered eternally in the one Word of the Father, who is Christ Jesus our Lord. May the grace of his silence be yours today.

ALWAYS AND EVERYWHERE GIVING THANKS

Feast of the Birthday of the Blessed Virgin Mary,
8 September 1992

> Father, all-powerful and ever-living God,
> we do well always and everywhere
> to give you thanks through Jesus Christ our Lord.

We repeat this phrase so often at the beginning of the preface of the Mass. It is, of course, particularly appropriate when we celebrate the gift God makes to us in the person of Our Lady, but it has a wider meaning too. We are invited to give thanks always and everywhere. In every time, in every circumstance, in every place.

Gratitude is the acknowledgement of a gift. We have so much to be thankful for. At every moment, God's creative love sustains us and all things in being. Things, persons, events, everything that is manifests his generous love and is ordained by his wisdom.

If holiness is the letting-be of God's life in and through us, its principal means is in identifying our will with that of God. Let us not limit this to obedience to his commands. This is essential, of course, but there is much more. We can positively will everything, always and everywhere, that God wills. Now God wills everything that is, the real here and now, as the real of all time.

This is perhaps the contemplatives' part: to breathe being into all that is by entering into and participating in God's creative love. One can thus feel something of the Father's joy in giving being. The Son, his Word, is of course the full expression of his joy. That is why our thanksgiving is always made through Jesus Christ who made the whole creation eucharistic in assuming our humanity and giving its praise a human voice.

But the kaleidoscope of creatures manifests that eternal wisdom that plays on the surface of the earth to the pleasure of the Father. Each smallest thing is a work of his love.

If I may share a personal experience, last week I created, or helped God create, West Sussex as far as my eyes could see from the Prior's verandah! Looking at the beautiful landscape, bathed in fresh morning

[38]

light, I let myself be drawn into it, become a part of it. I then willed with love each thing to be in naming it. I started with the easier things, the big ones: the downs, the sky, the green space of the fields. I then added in some trees, each with its own glistening beauty. Then, more difficult, with joy, some sweeping birds, and a frisky young calf and its mother.

I realised then that all these things mysteriously existed now in a way they had not before. Things are not just objects before us, they are what they are through the love and word that gives them being and meaning. I then turned my gaze nearer home and willed-to-be our house and each one of the persons in it, just as they are, as the Father wills each one with love. And I willed the circumstances of this moment of our individual and collective history, knowing them to be the working out of God's love and wisdom. We do not, we cannot always understand; we can always believe and will and give thanks. Even, perhaps in a more special way, we can know ourselves to be blessed in our poverty, our what may seem to us to be poverty. Christ is certainly there, leading us in his paradoxical paschal way, towards a newness that we cannot yet perceive. To accede to it, we must perhaps be stripped of some cherished garment or project; as a man, growing old, is stripped of his human power only to be made ready for the divine. For God alone is our land, Christ's mystery our way. Let us then hold on to nothing and go forward with Christ to the glory of the Father, our all-powerful and ever-living God, always and everywhere giving thanks, willing creatively all he wills, clothing all things with the beauty of his glory.

THE POOR OF CHRIST

Feast of St Bruno, 6 October 1992

The celebration of the feast of St Bruno is always an invitation to meditate on the meaning of our vocation. I would like to regard things today from a different angle. Often, perhaps, we centre too much on the figure of Bruno taken in isolation. He is spoken of as the founder of the Carthusian Order, yet it could be argued that this is not quite correct. He never intended to found an Order, as far as we know.

We tend to forget that he was one of a group of men, seven in all, who set forth together. Their life contained, from the beginning, a social interdependence, they formed a community. They were not a group of hermits accidentally living in proximity to one another. They were, and wanted to be, a community of hermits, the charity of their community life being the cement which held together their solitary life. And, at a very practical level, the community could not function without the complementary service of the Fathers and the Brothers.

Bruno, of course, held a central place in the community. He was the recognised head and an inspirational force, though what concrete form that took we do not really know. It was probably much less structured than nowadays, and based on Bruno's personal charism. The more juridical organisation described by Guigo came some years later, in part, no doubt, under the influence of Guigo's own turn of mind.

When Bruno was called to Italy, after only six years, the community faltered for a moment. The monks, disorientated without their leader, were dispersed. After two and a half years, however, they came back together again, drawn now not by the attractive force of the personality of Bruno but by their love for the contemplative values of the seeking of God in silence and solitude. This is a more mature community, inspired certainly by the example of Bruno, carrying on his legacy, yet more personally and without his presence.

We know their names. There was Master Lanuin, a man of delicate health whom Bruno named as his successor. (In passing, for many years this was the custom; rather than being elected by the community, the Prior was named by the outgoing Prior.) Then there were the two Stephens, Stephen of Bourg and Stephen of Die, both former canons of

St Ruf but not priests. The only priest among them was Hugh the chaplain. Finally there were the two converse Brothers, Andrew and Guerin.

We know a little about Master Lanuin because of his visit to Bruno in Calabria and the subsequent letter by Bruno to the Chartreuse, but of the others we know little more than their year of death. There would have been two or three on each side of choir. The chant would have been rustic, not all would have had good voices. I would not be surprised if one of them had a tendency to begin ahead of the rest! The liturgy, like the life, was very simple. They were a small group of unpretentious monks, who were known as the Pauperes Christi, the poor of Christ.

Yet the spiritual quality of these almost anonymous unsung men must have been very real, if we are to judge from the fecundity of the lineage issuing from it. They had their trials, of course, for theirs was necessarily the way of the cross. In the year 1132, 48 years after the foundation, an avalanche crushed the monastery, killing 7 of a community of about 15. The house was rebuilt with great difficulty at a site further down the valley, only to be burned down, and rebuilt, eight times in nine centuries. There were outstanding men from time to time across the centuries but basically it was the community, living and passing on its way of life, that lasted through time to our day.

One reason for drawing your attention to this is that the next General Chapter will discuss and try to formulate more clearly the role of the community in the formation of our young monks. This is intended to complete the documents on the role of the novice-master, and to give a more complete picture. The role of the novice-master is clearly very important, but it must be seen within the community. If the community does not fulfil its role, the novice-master alone can do nothing. What then is the role of the community? Why is it so important? Is it, finally, the community who is responsible for the formation of the young? What can we do, as a community, to fulfil our role better?

As you see, I am asking questions, not giving answers, for I would like you to reflect on this matter. In a month or two, we could perhaps share our thoughts and perhaps come up with some practical suggestions. I would like to be able to communicate to the General Chapter the opinions of the community, perhaps a written document. This will further help us to reflect together on our situation and discern better what God is trying to say to us, here and now.

[41]

May the spirit and grace of St Bruno enlighten our hearts, and give us joy and courage, as they did to the first small group of his companions, who were happy to be poor in Christ.

GOD'S POETRY

Feast of the Immaculate Conception of the Blessed
Virgin Mary, 8 December 1992

For me the feast of Our Lady's immaculate conception speaks of God's poetry. Beyond the weighty theology behind it, there is a poem, light and sparkling as the dew in the early morning sun. God the poet makes beauty from nothing. From the earth springs a perfect flower. Out of the dark humus of humanity's history warped by sin, God calls forth a being untouched by sin, who will be the mother of him who will save us all from sin.

It was as if God took his creation into his hands again and created, in a pure act of love, woman as she was intended to be. In truth the new Eve is a poetical creation, needing no justification other than that of her beauty. She is all grace and gratuity. Mary was preserved from sin, but the same grace can restore in Mary Magdalen the pristine clarity of the beginning – she too can become a poem to God's glory, a deep-hued flower of great beauty.

When we seem to ourselves to be in good spiritual shape, we easily pay lip-service to the truth that everything is grace. We believe in the doctor as long as we are in good health. On the contrary, it is precisely when we are painfully conscious of our weakness and sin that our belief in God gives him the greatest glory. All then is seen to be his work, and his alone. It is the style of God to make much of little.

Let us then not deplore but give thanks with Mary from the place of our lowliness, as individuals and as a community. Let us hold firmly to the belief that God's grace can make all things new. From the brave remnants of a community of men whose history is marked, as all human works are, by frailty, God can, if he wills, draw beauty, a poem, a pure flower. The less likely the matter, the poorer, the more is the artist tempted to show his worth. Coming after Christ, our humanity bears the marks of his suffering but the creative power of his grace is the same: the faith of Mary and the faith of Mary Magdalen is the same also. Let us celebrate the feast, then, in this spirit and in this hope. All things are possible to God and the works of the greatest poet are sudden works of beauty.

A BURNING CANDLE

Feast of the Presentation of the Lord, 2 February 1993

The symbol of a burning candle is at the heart of today's feast. I invite you simply to look at the candle before you and to let your mind flow freely between what you observe and what is symbolised.

Our gaze is drawn, I think, immediately to the tongue of flame, a moving column of light and heat. This represents, of course, Christ, the light of the world. In the radiance of this light, we see the face of the Father looking on us with love, sending his Son to redeem us and to give us communion in his own eternal life through the gift of the Holy Spirit, in whom we are sons. The heat the flame gives off is the warmth of Love.

The flame is communicated to us as one candle is lighted from another. The image comes to mind of the tongues of flame that descended on each of the apostles at Pentecost. And the spirit of charity can be communicated from one human heart to another, the surging of prayer from teacher to disciple.

You will notice that the flame is not part of the candle as such, i.e. the cylinder of tallow or wax with a wick through its centre. It must receive the flame from outside itself, but it can do so, it has the capacity to receive the flame of the Spirit. And what happens then? The flame is nourished on the inert wax and, bit by bit, consumes it and converts it into flame. In the terms of our analogy, the Spirit-flame that is given us transforms our heavy natural substance into Spirit, into love and light.

In one sense the candle loses itself, it is consumed by the flame, just as we must lose ourselves to become spiritual men, that is, animated by the Spirit. A reasonable candle might object to this process. He might point to the laborious effort of so many bees who had fabricated the wonderful substance of the wax. And had they not been programmed by God in his wisdom to do so? He might demand that his waxen nature be respected, that he be given a happiness suited to that nature. Why should he be sacrificed to this ephemeral flame and the folly of its prodigal giving of light to all without discrimination? O Lord, let me be, dull and opaque as I am. Must I die? 'If you wish to become light and love, then yes,' says Christ, 'you must follow me in my death to self so that my Spirit-flame may live and shine in you. Sacrifice is your hidden name, your anointed destiny. That is why you must be presented in God's temple.'

The Orthodox speak of this in terms of the light of Mount Tabor, the light that shone from Christ on the mountain of the Transfiguration. The idea is that in the saint, the man or woman totally animated by the Spirit of Christ, this same light should be visible, in some degree. And there have been persons in whom it indeed has.

I think we can regard the outward visibility as a charismatic event, only sometimes present according to the needs of the Church. But the inward transformation, the consuming presence of Christ's life and love, are of the essence of Christian life. Born of gift, it must become gift, gratuity. It will illuminate the whole house by being what it is, in whatever way, however unselfconsciously and ordinarily God gives it to be. The more ordinarily and unselfconsciously the better, in fact. The desert fathers would say that prayer is not perfect as long as it is conscious of itself as prayer.

This brings to mind another image dear to the desert fathers, who 'saw' prayer as a flame reaching up towards God. You know the story: Abbot Lot came to Abbot Joseph and said: 'Father, according as I am able, I keep my little rule, and my little fast, my prayer, meditation and contemplative silence: and according as I am able I strive to cleanse my heart of thoughts: now what more should I do?' The elder rose up in reply and stretched out his hands to heaven, and his fingers became like ten lamps of fire. He said: 'Why not be totally changed into fire?'

Or again, Abbess Syncletica: 'Our God is a consuming fire. We ought to light the divine fire in ourselves with labour and with tears.'

On this feast I wish you those tears so that the joy of Christ may shine in your prayer.

THE HEART'S TREASURE

First Sunday of Lent, 1993

Once again we enter the season of Lent. For me, it is always a season of grace, a sober invitation to come back to the essential, and to disencumber myself from the superficial and the transient. It is perhaps a sign of weakness to need this recall, but for me, I must admit it is necessary. In this perspective, the gospel of last Thursday struck me as very relevant. Listen to the first verses again.

> 'Do not store up for yourselves treasure on earth, where moth and rust destroy and thieves break in and steal; but store up treasure in heaven, where neither moth nor rust will destroy, nor thieves break in and steal. For where your treasure is, there will your heart be also.' (Matthew 6:19–21 REB)

Dry rot, rust, thieves breaking in – this surely concerns us!

Let us reflect a moment on the word 'treasure': treasure on earth that we should not store up, and treasure in heaven that we should. What is the treasure of my heart? The word 'treasure' denotes something considered valuable. Treasure on earth, in the gospel, seems to refer, firstly, to material things which can deteriorate or be stolen. Like our clock, for example! Or buildings, books, precious objects, machines, clothes, money, investments etc. Don't accumulate them beyond need, says Our Lord, or you will be burdened. Your heart will attach itself to them, you will become their slave, your worth will seem to be defined by what you possess, not by what you do and are.

Such is the way of the world, so often driven by a spirit of greed and selfishness. Prestige is measured often in terms of money and possessions. People seek to possess far beyond their reasonable needs, at the expense of others if necessary, for the power it brings, and the illusory sense of being somebody because one possesses something. God knows how much violence, crime and social injustice flows from this polluted source.

What is so harmful is the interior thing, not so much the objects themselves as the spirit of greedy possessiveness by which we appropriate for ourselves what is given for our use and to be shared by all. And let

[47]

us not be blind. In our circumstances, our hearts can be bound by that spirit of possessiveness towards things of no great intrinsic value. I think that one can include here non-material possessions such as prestige, power, reputation, honours. This is specially important for those called to contemplative prayer. Did not St John of the Cross insist that a single thread bound to a bird's foot is enough to prevent its soaring aloft? Remember the rich and pious young man whom Jesus looked at and loved and called to sell all and to come and follow him, a man called to be a cornerstone in the nascent Church. What an extraordinary opportunity offered to him! Instead of which, we see him go away, sad, for he had many possessions.

He could neither grasp nor follow the way of liberty and of love that Christ was teaching by his word and his life – he who did not consider equality with God a thing to be grasped, though he was the Son, but made himself nothing, humbling himself. The way to turn our heart towards God is by freeing it from the glue of possessiveness towards all that is not God. It is as simple as that. And we will then enjoy the happiness of the poor in spirit.

And the joy of Christ in us, for that is what it is. The love of God poured into our empty hearts will be a source of acts which build the eternal dwelling which is Christ's Body, in which all will find their peace. These are the treasures in heaven we are encouraged to store up. Not material things but 'whatever is true, noble, pure, lovely and honourable' (Philippians 4:8). Every act of love, humility, patience, faith, forgiveness, prayer, praise, adoration. Every good deed done and every suffering endured in Christ for his Body.

In the final analysis, we have one treasure only: 'Christ in us, the hope of glory' (Colossians 1:27). Any good deeds we may do, he does them in us (if not without us). 'By God's act you are in Christ Jesus: God has made him our wisdom, and in him we have our righteousness, our holiness, our liberation' (1 Corinthians 1:30 REB). Without him we can do nothing. In him, nothing is impossible.

May you ever more, this Lenten time, open your hearts to his power and peace and his joy in you.

FOR OUR SAKE HE OPENED HIS ARMS
ON THE CROSS

Feast of the Annunciation of the Lord, 25 March 1993

At the centre of every feast we celebrate, there is the Mass, there is Christ's sacrifice rendered present and active in and through the eucharistic celebration. This is the still point transcending time and space, from which all our spiritual movement derives. Each morning we are born again of God's creative goodness and we praise him for his works, we adore him in his majesty. Each day we are washed in the blood of Christ and made clean. Each day we are freed and enabled for the works of love, as Christ loves us. We bring, each day, our concrete life to be consecrated to the Father, so that all our acts may be ordered to him and made holy in his charity.

The image before us is that of Christ, who 'for our sake opened his arms on the cross'. It is thus that 'he put an end to death and revealed the resurrection' (Eucharistic Prayer). This is the image I would like to leave you with today: that of Christ, his arms opened in total vulnerability, giving himself without reserve to the Father and to us, breathing out his Spirit to the Father and on us, open to receive and embrace us. Immobile, fixed to the cross that he freely assumed for us, he is, paradoxically, wholly ascension to the Father in obedience, praise, trust and abandonment. He is love, to the end. And thus is he resurrection.

Each day, when we participate in the Eucharist, our lives are signed with the cross. We open ourselves to be drawn into the movement of self-emptying love and sacrifice. We offer our being and life to be transformed in the image of Christ. We are the bread to be consecrated. This is our essential Christian priesthood, common to every one of us by baptism, for whose service the ministerial priesthood exists. And it is by becoming thus the Body of Christ that we are bonded into one.

Let us each day open our hearts to the full force of Christ's Spirit emanating from the sacrifice of the Mass. The essential is already present in Mary's 'yes' at the Annunciation. Through the whole liturgy of this time, Christ will take us by the hand and initiate us more and more into the mystery of his love, so that we too may put an end to death in ourselves and in the world, and reveal the resurrection.

GOD'S LIFE IN OUR MORTAL VEINS

Easter Sunday, 1993

For some reason my mind keeps coming back to the Eucharist these days. It is after all, the sacrament of the Paschal Mystery, its symbolic representation. Through this simple rite, Jesus tried to make his disciples grasp the meaning of what was to happen.

It is so simple and so profound. Jesus knows he is about to die. He gathers his disciples about him and eats with them, Judas included, remember; his presence is essential: Jesus will give his life for him perhaps in a special way. Christ's lonely journey into the ultimate stripping of death concerns them all, even to their weakness and their sin. He will not leave them, he will be with them as a leaven of healing and spirit-life. Let us listen to the terse narrative in the second Eucharistic Prayer:

> Before he was given up to death, a death he freely accepted,
> he took bread and gave you (Father) thanks.
> He broke the bread, gave it to his disciples and said:
> Take this, all of you and eat it:
> this is my body which will be given up for you.
> When supper was ended, he took the cup. Again he gave you
>   thanks and praise,
> gave the cup to his disciples and said: Take this all of you and
>   drink from it:
> this is the cup of my blood, the blood of the new and everlasting
>   covenant.
> It will be shed for you and for all, so that sins may be forgiven.
> Do this in memory of me.

This is the meaning of my sacrifice, Jesus is saying, and this is the way you must follow if you are to love as I have loved, if you wish to enter into the life of the resurrection. Let us look at things very simply from this angle today, enumerating some of the qualities of life and love of which Christ gives us here the example. What are they?

- Liberty: with conscious freedom to give our life, the heart's choice beyond all exterior or interior constraint.
- Total gift: not this or that, but our life itself, all we have, be it but a widow's mite.
- Grateful acceptance: of our humanity and of all creation in a spirit of thanksgiving and of praise. We take the bread and wine that symbolise them and we give thanks.
- Sharing: we break the bread and we give it: the bread of our human lives, our hearts, our thoughts, our time, our dreams, our disappointments, our pain, our faults, our hopes. Take, eat, this is my body.
- Solidarity: This is my body given up for you. Christ took his place among us, as it were, beside us. He did not look down upon us from a position of invulnerable superiority. He accepted us, each and all as we are in truth, and tied his lot to ours. So doing he could apply the healing gift of the Spirit to our very real wounds from within and restore us to God's friendship. 'This is the cup of my blood, the blood of the new and everlasting covenant. It will be shed for you and for all, so that sins may be forgiven.'

In this pardon, from this covenant, the Church and our community are born. Only in shared pardon and in communion with Christ can it continue to exist. In practice, this is a hard saying: it is not easy to accept a real solidarity with each and every one of my brothers, not only with the amenable, the gifted and the well-disposed towards me, but also with the less agreeable, the less gifted, and the less well-disposed, even hostile. Or I accept only those parts of their personalities that I approve of, as if a person could be divided. It is hard not to exclude from our hearts through arrogance or defensiveness or judgement. We religious are far too prone to sit in judgement on others, even though we know in our hearts that we are no better ourselves. Let us learn of Christ to judge no one, to exclude no one, to accept as a precious gift each of our brothers and sisters. This is not 'charity', it is their right in Christ. We must learn to suffer, not only from them, as may sometimes happen, but with them; to sustain them by our pardon, to carry them in our heart's prayer: to help them carry their cross, from which they are the first to suffer, rather than pharisaically to condemn their weaknesses. Community implies sacrifice, it is founded in the cup of Christ's blood. Remember this when you drink of this chalice. The General Chapter will be studying the role of the community in formation. Beyond any exterior thing, it lies, or so it seems to me, in this real solidarity in Christ's love. All the rest will follow.

And it is thus that we will know that we are risen in Christ, by the Spirit that has been poured out in our hearts, God's Life in our mortal veins. Already we are risen in Christ: in a hidden way, the eternal realities are present. Sacramentally we see them and in faith we try to live them. As in Christ's humanity the divinity was truly present but unseen to human eyes, so now is the life of the resurrection present in us, here and now to be lived, but under the veil of our humanity, shining obscurely through, often, in a strange way, through the wounds of our hearts.

We come back in full circle to the image of Christ crucified, but now transfigured, bearing the crown of his triumph, as the Eastern Fathers loved to portray him.

I wish you the fullness of his joy this day.

THE CENTRE OF STILLNESS

Pentecost Sunday, 1993

The General Chapter is an experience of much community life and activity. In preparing for it, I happened on a book about Dag Hammarskjöld, a Swede who was Secretary General of the United Nations in the 1950s. Though plunged in intense and important activity, he was a great Christian and man of prayer who sought the source of that activity in the inner soul.

He constructed, in the middle of the enormous United Nations building in New York, a meditation room. This room contains only a huge block of Swedish iron ore struck by a sloping shaft of light, symbolising the light of the spirit which gives life to matter, the block of Swedish iron representing the cornerstone of faith.

In a leaflet for visitors, he describes the room in this way:

> We all have within us a centre of stillness, surrounded by silence. This house, dedicated to work and debate in the service of peace, should have one room dedicated to silence in the outward sense, and stillness in the inner sense. It has been the aim to create in this small room a place where doors may be opened to the infinite lands of thought and prayer. People of many faiths will meet here, at one in the utter simplicity of the universal symbols used. . . . There is an ancient saying that the sense of a vessel is not in its shell but in its void. So it is with this room. It is for those who come here to fill the void with what they find in their centre of stillness.

We find there echoes of Thomas à Kempis and a venerable mystical tradition. It is not difficult for us to apply what he says to our own vocation: we could regard the monastery itself, each cell, and finally the heart of each monk as concentric circles around the still point of the inflowing Spirit.

First, the monastery as a whole. In our busy world and in the Church beset by so many immediate needs, the Charterhouse has the mission to be a centre of stillness where human beings speak with God and use their voices to adore and praise his glory. The buildings themselves are grouped around the church and the invisible presence of Christ, figuring a community born of a shared solitude, overspilling in simple fraternity. In a word, it is a place of lived prayer. This is our essential witness.

Within the monastery, the cell delimits the personal space of each one, a space to be with God in silence and peace, according to the grace each one has received.

All this, however, is of little avail, if it is but an exterior thing. The solitude and silence must be interiorised. It is in the inner cell of the heart that the Lord is met. It is to the heart that God speaks, it is from within that his Spirit is poured forth, a Spirit of truth and love that bonds us to him and gives us to live, to know and to love, in some measure, as he lives, knows and loves. And in this one Spirit we are united to all our brothers and sisters in Christ.

All our concern is to open our hearts and minds to God's Spirit, to allow ourselves to be introduced into God's life, beyond anything we can conceive. To this end are necessary the faith and interior silence of one who receives God's Word in his heart and lets his mind be moulded by it. There is need too of interior poverty, the letting go of our hold on self, of our desire to be in control, in order to be begotten by the Spirit as sons and daughters of God, empowered to love in the measure of Christ. This emptying of self is the ultimate cross in our lives, but, lived in joyful faith, it is also the hidden life of the resurrection, Christ living in us.

I understand all this of 'the centre of stillness surrounded by silence' of which Dag Hammarskjöld speaks. With him, I do believe that only from this centre can peace come to the world, to our community and to each one of us in his solitude. Let us then do what we can to enter into this still place of love and truth to receive the gift of God himself. At peace, in Christ, we will then be sources of peace for all. That it may be so, may the Father give you all of the abundance of his Spirit through his Son this day.

SILENCE, THE LANGUAGE OF THE WORLD TO COME

Feast of the Assumption of the Blessed Virgin Mary,
15 August 1993

To introduce today's feast, I would like to make some reflections on the subject of silence. As Isaac the Syrian says, somewhere, 'Words are the language of this world, silence is the language of the world to come.' The Assumption points directly to that world and it seems appropriate to speak of silence on this occasion.

What is silence? Why is it held in such esteem by spiritual people of all religions? Silence is far more than the absence of sound. It is a complex human reality and can be a precious means of entry into the spiritual world. Rightly understood, silence is rich and positive. It is, perhaps, the ultimate modesty of the mind before the mystery of being. And have you ever remarked how the first shock of real beauty renders us silent?

There is exterior silence and interior silence. The monastery is, or should be, a place of at least relative silence in the sense of the absence of unnecessary noise and agitated movement. We are less assaulted by harsh sounds; rather we are soothed by the mostly harmonious sounds of nature, and bells and our Gregorian chant. This pacifies our sensibility and refines it. A heightened awareness is a common experience in solitude and affects all the senses, for they are all linked together. In silence we are more vividly aware of colour, and perfume and touch, because we are more present to ourselves. And little by little, we become attuned to the breathing spaces of silence between the sounds, as it were, like an underlying melody, not exactly 'heard', and yet somehow perceived, something that can take the character of a presence.

Silence begets an attitude of listening; a recollected capacity to receive the manifold communications of being through the doors of the senses, which yet go beyond the sensual to become mediators of a communion of our mind and spirit with what is. The artist, the philosopher, the praying person may perceive or, at least, express in different words

diverse aspects of this reality, but all have need of silence, receptivity and awareness.

There is an interior silence which is essential if the exterior silence is to have its effect. A silence of the mind and of the heart. A calm mind, not forever chattering to itself, capable of listening, of receiving what it does not already know. And a purified and unified heart, not agitated and torn this way and that by its passions and appetites, clamouring for their satisfaction and deaf to all else. These must be cleansed by the tears of compunction, transformed by the fire of compassion, meekness and forgiveness and brought into the order of love: love of God, and love of ourselves and our brothers and sisters in God. When God is the centre of our universe and not our little egotistical self, then will there be liberty and peace within us, then will there be real interior silence, that purity of heart to which it is promised to see God.

This is an ideal towards which we aspire and, hopefully, tend throughout our life. We know the way because Christ has shown it to us. The way of the beatitudes, of emptying of self to let God be and live and love in us. The Father has sent us his Word in order to lead us into his eternal beatitude. Paradoxically, the fullness of his Word in us begets silence; silence of self-emptying, silence of love and adoration. It is in God that we see the real nature of this silence of adoration, for in him all is light, pure being in act, total intelligence in his Word, total communion in his Spirit, totally one without division or fragmentation.

Our words are many, manifesting the limited and partial understanding we have of the myriad aspects of created being. Our mind, as it were, takes the form of each concept we make, then passes on, its capacity unfulfilled, for it is indeed infinite. But in the silence of adoration, God opens a window on the infinite and by love draws the created spirit obscurely into the mystery of his transcendence. Obscurely, for he must divest it of the limitations of any created form. Here the soul can know only in not-knowing. The Word is begotten in her in silence, God's silence which is eternal beatitude.

This is the beginning on earth of that life which is our hope in Christ, and into which the Blessed Virgin has entered already, body and soul. May each of us attain to it at the appointed time. That is my prayer for you today.

IN PRAISE OF BEGINNINGS

Feast of the Birthday of the Blessed Virgin Mary,
8 September 1993

But I, being poor, have only my dreams; . . .
Tread softly because you tread on my dreams.

W. B. Yeats

Life, as we know it, is a constant succession of beginnings. The mark of God's work is to make all things new, even that which was deformed and distorted.

Let us look at some images of beginnings so as to put ourselves, as it were, in tune with God's Spirit. There is the hypothetical Big Bang: the immense variety of cosmic matter issuing out from a single point of intense density, giving birth to time and space.

There is spring: nature stretching forth its new green shoots to the sun. There is the break of dawn, a fresh day setting out with dewy locks on its ordained course.

Then there are human beginnings. The apparently random lottery of conception. Birth itself. The first smile. The first words spoken, the first steps taken, entering into school, starting to work, perhaps falling in love, waking up each morning to the glory of another day.

And there are spiritual beginnings. The awesome gift of baptism, the beginning of a new life in God. The eternal newness of the Eucharist: always the same, Christ's unique sacrifice, always new, making of each successive moment the sacrament of his Spirit; assuming, transforming time. The sacrament of reconciliation, renewing by the grace of pardon what has been damaged by our falls, setting us free to live and love in him again. Beyond the celebration of the sacrament, our attitude towards ourselves and others should be inspired by that of God towards us, for we are inconstant and weak.

The sacraments of marriage, of healing, and of order are all entries into new modes of life. Every time Christ touches us there is new life, a new beginning. He is indeed the Lord of the resurrection. For our part, we must be poor enough to receive the newness of his gifts, for the Spirit is infinitely creative. We must not cling to the past, good or bad.

It is but to cling to an image of ourselves and shut ourselves off from the abounding vitality of the Father. Rather we must have the courage, in faith, to let go of all that encumbers us and to dare to trust and hope in God alone. Then will the beginnings of Christ be realised in our lives. In him every day, every moment can be a new beginning, traversed by a spark of his creative energy. 'Your joy no one will take from you' (John 16:22).

I wish you that joy that showed itself so gracefully in the Virgin Mary whose birthday we celebrate today.

'LET ALL GOD'S GLORY THROUGH'

*Feast of the Immaculate Conception of the Blessed
Virgin Mary, 8 December 1993*

I like to enter into the spirit of the liturgical season and let myself be carried along each year, ever deeper. Now, at first sight, the feast of the Immaculate Conception might seem to be something of an intrusion, or at best a parenthesis. What has this feast to do with Advent, which is ordained wholly towards the coming of Christ? In fact, if one looks more closely, it sheds a precious light on the coming of Christ, on the Incarnation of the Word of God in Jesus, and on his coming to be in our hearts and in our lives.

Essentially, the feast of the Immaculate Conception celebrates the proximate first step of Christ's coming. It says that the mother of Jesus is God's work, is totally his doing. Mary's bearing of Jesus is not just an event in her life, however important, it is her reason for being what she is. She is pure. Her being and her task are one. As G. M. Hopkins puts it, Mary

> This one work had to do –
> Let all God's glory through.

Now, if you will permit me a rather bold comparison, I wonder if we cannot speak of something analogous to an immaculate conception in each one of us, in the sense of a place deep in our hearts, which is God's own work and which is not defiled even by our failings and our sins? A place where our being and our actions coincide, so that we become what we really are under God's creative touch. Is not this the 'place of God' of which Eastern spirituality speaks and which is deemed to be the seat of pure prayer? The coming of Christ will be realised in our hearts when we are situated in this place, when we are begotten in Christ and his life-Spirit shines through our being and our acts.

Because our life moves through time, and our being expresses itself in fragmentary acts, there will be moments of conception, of beginnings that will be, more or less, God's own work in us. Obviously, it is of great importance to be able to recognise these moments and to correspond to their grace. Our problem in life often is to discern in our choices and actions what is of God and what is not from God but rather from evil or from the flawed source of our own ignorance and self-seeking.

Every discernment will be unique, of course, but we will expect to find certain common signs bearing the mark of Mary and of Christ.

- The sign of total willingness in faith, as in Mary who, though conscious of her own poverty and unable to comprehend how God's plan could humanly be realised in her, yet gives her yes to the action of the overshadowing Spirit.
- The sign of hiddenness, of humility and of the joy of obedience in abandonment to the Father, as in Christ.
- The sign of charity, of the love that gives itself in sacrifice for us, for all people.
- The sign of the cross, of contradiction and of difficulties. The servant will be no better treated than the master. The self-emptying Christ is often more truly present in our weaknesses, even in pardon to our sins, than in our apparent strengths. The real works of God are marked by the foolishness of God which is the opposite of the wisdom of this world, wholly occupied with having the biggest slice of the cake possible and quite willing to trample on anybody in its way to get it.
- The sign of kenotic poverty, the non-possession of God's gifts and works, the relinquishing of all claims to justice before God.
- The sign of peace, the tranquillity of God's order.
- When we empty ourselves of our little selves, even though there seems to be nothing left, Christ can come wholly into our hearts, begetting our true self as children of God. Then it is that the Spirit conceives his acts in us with the audacity of his inspiration. Then, like Mary, we have but one work – the Father's – to do and let all God's glory through.

CONSECRATION

Feast of the Presentation of the Lord, 2 February 1994

I would like to dwell on one simple aspect of today's feast: the fact that it concerns the consecration of a child to God. This invites us to reflect on what happens in every consecration to God by a person.

Perhaps one could say that it is always a child that is consecrated. It is the child in us who has dreams of things that do not yet exist. The child sees a beauty and is caught up in the wonder of it. He, or she, is easily inflamed by an ideal. For him the boundary between what is, here and now, and what could be is very tenuous. He will believe the promise. He will take God literally at his word and not count the cost.

Is he just an escapist, living in a world of imagination? This may be the case when there is no real commitment and nothing of self is given. At other times, the child manifests the creative vitality of the Spirit. He is, in us, the real visionary that sets out in quest of the holy Grail, as we have perceived it. We can never gainsay him. We can, of course, silence him, kill him in the name of prudence, or of fear, or of being sensible, or of being like everyone else. The wasting effect of time and the hard school of our failures may urge us to do so, but, if we do, only the empty husk of ourselves will remain.

But surely the child's dream is unreasonable! What does he know of the limits of human nature ('I am as I am'), of the wear and tear of time, of the unforeseen turns and twists of the events of our histories?

In reply to this difficulty, we have to remember that our dream is the reflection of God's dream. We are God's dream. He it is who first conceives the life he would give us. Sanctifying grace is the radical gift of its communication. The entire being of the baptised is made holy by the outpouring of the Holy Spirit. It is in the baptised as a seed of Christ-life, vitally pushing towards expression in his or her life. This is the hidden source of our dream. God has first loved us. One sees this most clearly in the case of infant baptism. The commitment to God is made by others in the child's name. The adult will have to ratify it or not in due course. It is also seen when the adult-child feels called to give a more specific form to this consecration in marriage or religious life or priesthood or whatever. This may involve a promise or a vow to God

[64]

concerning his or her future years. He does not know, he cannot know what lies in store for him, or how he will change throughout his life. He knows himself and various motivations only in part. An area essentially unknown opens before his liberty.

This is of the essence of human liberty, that it does not preclude engaging a person's future. For it is not our limited vision that is important. What counts is God's vision which is truth and enfolds all time, and God's will which is love and wisdom. The child-adult's leap into the unknown is an immense act of confidence and trust in God who is perceived as calling to himself.

The one so called does not seek to impose a preconceived ideal image of himself. Rather he radically relinquishes any such pretension by plunging his will into that of God and abandoning himself to his Love and Wisdom. He wills God as God wills himself, and himself as he is in God's own willing. At the limit, he need will only God.

And so his particular history unfolds with its ups and downs, its joys and sorrows. He lets himself be led in the paths of the Lord according to the often strange thoughts of God as he enters into the mystery of God. He will inevitably have to bear his cross as he follows Christ. He will appear to be a fool in the eyes of others and in truth he will be one. He will be led out of himself to find himself. He will be born anew in order to become himself. Finally we believe that he will attain to the ineffable mystery of the Father's eternal love.

Today, let the fragile flame of the candle, lit from the Christ-light that came into the world as a child, symbolise our dream and our hope.

TO SEEK GOD TRULY

First Sunday of Lent, 1994

The only thing that St Benedict asked of the aspirant monk was that he sought God truly. It is, perhaps, all we should ask of any monk, whatever his age or experience. To seek God truly, and not some other thing, however legitimate, is rare, and difficult to maintain throughout a lifetime. In fact, it is possible only at the price of a continuing purification of our initial seeking and a progressive abandoning of what I like to call our household gods, the images and idols we adore or fear in place of God in his truth. I am constantly appalled at the disfiguring masks we project on to God from our own private chamber of horrors. What patience God must have that so few succeed in breaking free of their inner fantasies to see and meet him as he is! That is, of course, a whole programme.

What is it to seek God truly? It is to love God, at least with a love of desire, to let ourselves be drawn to him as our sovereign good. The perception of his goodness may be very obscure but it is enough to reveal to us the depths of our heart which can never be satisfied with any created good. We desire to know him, to enter into conscious communion with him, in some way to participate in the fullness of his being. We are fascinated by his mystery and drawn by his beauty, and so set out to seek him.

To seek him is to turn away from many human goods, at least for those who are called to follow Christ in a way of poverty, chastity and obedience in order to be more radically free for God. This sacrifice is essentially priestly, for it flows from the priestly character imparted by the baptismal consecration in Christ and has a redemptive value for all humankind. Whatever the concrete form it takes, the seeking of God will imply a commitment of our whole person, body and soul, mind and heart.

To seek God truly is, as far as possible, to give him our undivided attention, to receive and to meditate on his Word, to contemplate his works. It is to let ourselves be taught the mystery of his love, to learn to love in him in our turn. It is to become thus a person, a real subject

[67]

in exchange with him who is the supreme subject. It is to be free at last in Christ whose word makes us free.

To seek God truly is to empty ourselves so that Christ, the divine face of our humanity, may live in us. To seek God truly is to trust in God, to will God willing, in all things. It is to seek him in sickness and in health, in wealth and in poverty, in light and in darkness, in fidelity and in infidelity (ours – God is always faithful), in good-doing and in sin, in strength and in weakness, in fear lest having him we have nothing else, in hope that in having him we will have all else, in love of what we do not know, yet obscurely intuit, in letting go of what is behind, not looking back, in communion with others and in solitude, in doubt and in simplicity, in anger and in meekness, in vanity and in humility, in healing and in hoarding our wounds, in trouble and in peace, in truth and in falsehood, in our dying in our mortal frame and in our being begotten as children of God.

We seek because we have been found. So seek that you may find. This grace I ask for you all this Lenten time.

THE BEGINNING AND THE END

Feast of the Annunciation of the Lord, 25 March 1994

I would like to share something more personal with you today. Yesterday I received a letter from a young woman in her early twenties telling me of the death of her mother who had died, rapidly and unexpectedly, of cancer. She wrote to me because she knew that her mother (her name is Thérèse) and I had been intimate friends before I, as she put it, entered the Brotherhood. I was very touched for, in fact, I had been courting Thérèse, and if my life had followed a normal path, I would perhaps have married her and the young woman writing to me (her name is Elisabeth) would have been my daughter. The Lord had other ideas, and I made a radical turn around and entered the monastic life. He had to break my leg to get the message through my thick head, of course. I have never regretted it and there was no going back.

Thérèse, in due course, got married, had children and got on with a normal life, with some writing of poetry and plays on the side. After some years, when she felt she was not a 'temptation' for me, she wrote and kept me informed of the events of her life. She even entrusted her family to the spiritual care of my prayer in a very real way.

The news of her death both brought back a whole part of my life and also a sort of picture of how it could have unfolded in its beginning and in its end. Thérèse was a good woman and lived a good life. Death has put its seal on that life which can now be seen in its entirety. My life could have been more or less parallel, but had not been. Yet the life that I do live will have its entirety and its end.

It is death that interrogates me. I cannot speak from experience of it. No one can, except the risen Christ. I know the emptiness of words addressed to a person facing the ultimate solitude of his or her own death. I, like each one of you, will have to pass through that door. I refuse to indulge in facile intellectualisations, but I know I do have faith, and it is God's gift, in the ultimate victory of life, which is not taken away but transformed into a deeper and fuller life. Our life on earth is a slow maturing of that life in us, an opening of our selves, more and more, to its vitality, an abandoning of ourselves to the mystery of love and light beyond our understanding, an ever more pure willing of God

[69]

in us. I do believe and hope that we will be reunited with those we love in a communion of persons that transcends the limits and partial nature of all communion on earth. That joy no one will take from us for all eternity.

You may be wondering what this has to do with the feast of the Annunciation. The connection is that which exists between the beginning and the end. In the Annunciation we see the beginning of Christ's life in Mary's womb. In our death, Christ's life in us comes to its full flowering into the world of the resurrection.

I ask your prayers for Thérèse and her family. I pray that you all may enter ever more fully into the mystery of Christ's life and death during this coming week and, more importantly, at the hour of your death.

LIGHT OUT OF DARKNESS

Easter Sunday, 1994

The icon you see before you shows Christ resplendent in light. The icons of Eastern Christendom portray the Resurrection, not as in medieval Western painting showing Christ stepping out of a tomb, but as Christ triumphing over the imprisoning powers of darkness. In a shimmering aura of glory, with hands outstretched, he draws Adam and Eve, representing all humanity, from death to life, from the old order to the new. The prisoners are set free, the demons are fallen, and life reigns. He descended into hell but rose again victorious, leaving the bars of hell shattered behind him.

At first glance our icon seems to express the same thing. But look more closely. Behind the resplendent Christ a mountain is profiled. And at his feet there are some huddled forms. In fact, this is not an icon of the risen Christ. It is an icon of the Transfiguration. The ease with which one confuses them is itself significant. In a sense, they both speak of the same reality but caught at different moments of time. In the Transfiguration the divine life of Christ shines through his body, transfiguring it by anticipation. Christ has not yet suffered, died and been raised to life, but the principle of the risen life, the Holy Spirit, is already present and active. In a way the life of the Resurrection can be seen here in a more visible way than after the paschal events. For the Resurrection cannot really be represented. It belongs to the realm of mystery, beyond our ken and our direct experience, whereas this veiled bodily presence, situated in the trajectory of time and mortal life, this we know, for it is what we ourselves live. One could say that the Transfiguration is the icon of the Resurrection given to us by God himself.

It has also the advantage of bringing the Resurrection into contact with the ordinary human condition in time with its sufferings, obscurities, crosses and joys. We follow Christ in faith and in hope, through death to life. Here I would like to let St Paul speak. He expresses what I mean far better than I could.

It is the God who said, 'Let light shine out of darkness', who has shone in our hearts to give the light of the knowledge of the glory of God in the face of Jesus Christ.

But we have this treasure in clay jars, so that it may be made clear that this extraordinary power belongs to God and does not come from us. We are afflicted in every way, but not crushed; perplexed, but not driven to despair; persecuted, but not forsaken; struck down, but not destroyed; always carrying in the body the death of Jesus, so that the life of Jesus may also be made visible in our bodies. . . . We know that the one who raised the Lord Jesus will raise us also with Jesus, and will bring us with you into his presence. . . . So we do not lose heart. Even though our outer nature is wasting away, our inner nature is being renewed day by day. For this slight momentary affliction is preparing us for an eternal weight of glory beyond all measure, because we look not at what can be seen but at what cannot be seen; for what can be seen is temporary, but what cannot be seen is eternal . . . We wish not to be unclothed but to be further clothed, so that what is mortal may be swallowed up by life. He who has prepared us for this very thing is God, who has given us the Spirit as a guarantee. (2 Corinthians 4:6–9, 14, 16–18; 5:4–5 NRSV)

A FINGER POINTING

Feast of the Birthday of John the Baptist, 24 June 1994

The figure of John the Baptist is a powerful symbol of the eremitical life. He stands before us stark and clear-cut, his whole being a finger pointing towards an invisible reality. Solitude is his milieu of life, silence the mantle he wears. What is silence, what is solitude for the contemplative?

Solitude is not isolation, the cutting off of oneself from others. It is rather a mystery of communion, a being-with in a deeper way; a being with God, with Christ and, potentially, with all people. It is a being grafted into the vine of Christ so as to become one with his body which is the Church. It is being enabled to intercede from within a real solidarity with all people in Christ. It is a being caught up into the paschal mystery of his redemptive love.

Likewise silence is not the mere absence of speech. It is listening to God, receiving the word he communicates to us in his creation and in the history of salvation. It is entering into communion with his superabundant life, a life of mutual knowledge and love. It is speaking with God as one would speak with a friend, with words and without words at that point where all the partial words come together in the reality of pure communion. It is this silence that animates and gives substance to the song of our adoration and praise, for it is, as it were, the hidden presence of the unique Word in whom the Father, through the Spirit of his Love, says eternally all that was, that is and that will be.

Our life, like that of John the Baptist, should be a living witness to the reality of God through such a silence and such a solitude. May it be so a little more each day, and especially this day, for all of you, in Christ our Lord.

A HIDDEN NAME

Receiving the Habit as Converse Brother,
Feast of the Assumption of the Blessed Virgin Mary,
15 August 1994

Receiving the monastic habit signifies the entry into the monastic life. You are crossing a threshold that will radically change you. The habit signifies Christ. In putting it on, you are being clothed in Christ, not just the body but the heart and soul as well. Your task is to realise this, to make it real by the grace of God, in your whole being and life.

The fact that this should happen on the feast of the Assumption of Our Lady is symbolic. In Our Lady we see the fulfilment of our spiritual journey. Just as she entered, body and soul, into the definitive life won for us by Christ, so, hopefully, will each one of us. During our life, we will try to cultivate the seed of life that is given to us, letting all our being, our attitudes, our acts be informed by the Spirit, opening ourselves in joyful trust and thanksgiving to the outpouring of love and light that is the life of God. This is our goal.

The way is Christ, being conformed to his death and to his life. In choosing the Carthusian life, you have chosen to follow Christ completely in response to the special and personal call he has addressed to you. He has called you by your name. We each have a hidden name that designates the inmost part of our being which is turned towards and, as it were, in immediate contact with God. This name will be revealed only in the beatific vision. The name we bear in this world can, to some extent, signify it, at least pointing towards the way we are to follow.

Your name is particularly apt for the life you have chosen, that of a converse Brother. We know little of Joseph. There were dramatic moments in his life, of course: Bethlehem, the flight into Egypt, the temple episode, but my feeling at least is that for the essential Joseph, the body and substance of his life was in the ordinary, simple, working, family life in Nazareth. The child and his mother depended on him for food, a home, love, basic education, a place in the social fabric of their village. He seems to have been a simple man, hidden in his ordinariness, 'only' Joseph the carpenter. He did not have any part in Christ's public life of preaching. It would seem he was dead by then. More profoundly, his contribution to Christ's work was situated at another level, at the level of his personal relationship with Christ, what he gave of himself to the human person of Jesus. We know how important this is in the development of the personality. Judging by the fruits, he loved much and wisely.

As a Brother, your contribution to the body of Christ which is the Church will have some of the same characteristics. It will be simple yet essential. It will be very much incarnated, yet the fruit of the Spirit. It will be concerned with the material well-being of a small group of Christ's disciples, yet it will be Jesus whom you will serve in them. Its truth will be plain to see, verifiable in a very concrete obedience, effort, humility and charity, yet it will receive all its energy from within, from a deep, personal love of Christ and a willingness to carry the burdens of his cross as they present themselves in the vicissitudes of real life. Prayer and work will be inextricably interwoven in the silent world of the monastery, not the silence of an absence of life, but the harmonious silence of well-ordered activity. Like Mary and Joseph you will follow the way, not of riches or power, but the humble hidden path of Nazareth and so enter, day by day, more deeply into kingdom of God.

Relying on the intercession of Our Lady and of St Joseph will you thus follow Christ to the Father?

'I AM MAKING ALL THINGS NEW'

Feast of St Bruno, 6 October 1994

Vatican 2 invited the religious orders to a renewal of their lives, on the one hand by returning to their true sources, namely the Word of God and the charism of the founder, and on the other hand by correctly reading the signs of the times and responding creatively to the needs of the contemporary world. There is therefore a looking back and a looking forward, an opening to the Spirit that animates our Order for all time as a spring nourishes a river in all its length, and a listening to this same Spirit as it speaks to us through the conditions and events of the historic moment in which we live. It is the constant dialogue between old and new, the creative adaptation of the living social organism that characterises a life at once faithful to its original identity and capable of giving itself new forms and ways of being as historically required.

This implies change and change is threatening to a venerable institution. It is a going into the unknown and unproved. By reaction, there is a risk of an institution refusing all change, however necessary, and becoming calcified, a museum of fossils from the past, completely out of touch with the times. There is the corresponding risk of an institution losing contact with its living tradition and its past and modelling itself, without discernment, on the values and manners of contemporary society that are rarely inspired by the gospel of Christ. We have then to go forward, without falling into one or other of these extremes, in a paschal faith in God's loving providence, humbly prepared to let go of whatever may be an obstacle to the inflowing life of Christ and the creative newness of his Spirit.

Renewal involves three principal stages:

1 A perception that things are not perfect, that something needs to be done.
2 A questioning of existing attitudes and structures with all the anxiety and pain and insecurity that this involves. There is an impression of chaos, a passage through a desert.
3 A formulation of a new understanding of the life and goals of the

Institute and a finding of more adequate attitudes and structures, expressing a newfound consensus and integration.

In the light if this, where should we situate the Carthusian Order thirty years after the Council? I think that, with the rest of the Church, we are still in the desert period though with some first-fruits of the promised land in view. Renewal concerns more than ideas and documents, it demands a change of the attitudes of the heart and personal conversion. We can have very strong resistance, more or less conscious, to it.

There can be the denial that there is a problem, that anything needs to be changed. This was the attitude of a certain number in the Order, particularly among the older monks at the time of the Council. The call for renewal came from without, not so much from the Carthusian grass roots. They failed to realise that they could not isolate themselves from the global situation of the Church and the world. One can readily understand how difficult it was and is for them to assimilate the new understanding of itself proposed by the Church, at least at the level of the heart.

The Order as such sought to be obedient to the Spirit of Christ speaking to it through the Council. There were consultations of the members of the Order, commissions, meetings, experimentation in some areas, and finally the new Statutes that sought to codify the effort of renewal. Further experimentation was discouraged, without it being possible to revert to the legislative immobility of the pre-Council days. What was the result? Much that was obsolete in the observance was dropped. Solitude was favoured by restoring the primitive balance of liturgy in church and in cell. The texts of the liturgy were enriched and some degree of vernacular introduced while still maintaining the preponderance of Latin and Gregorian chant. In general, more was left to the responsibility of the individual monk than to detailed legislation, and the exercise of authority was envisaged from a more pastoral point of view. At the level of the Order more authority was devolved to the Houses, and the General Chapter began to function in a more corporate way. A serious effort was made to improve the formation process. The status of the Brothers as fully monks was affirmed. Active participation in choir and the habitation of a hermitage became possible for the Brothers who desired it.

Are we nearer to the primitive simplicity and authenticity of the life of our Fathers? At least the possibility is there. So, everything is fine? Hardly, yet. The communities of the Order, in general, are ageing. There is recruitment in the last decade or two but the perseverance is poor, the problems in the field of formation more and more complex. The shape of the future is uncertain.

Our own house illustrates this well. We must admit a real poverty and precariousness as a community, as well as a considerable cultural distance separating us from the contemporary scene. To enter into the Charterhouse nowadays for a young man represents a sort of emigration. This is not entirely negative. Monastic life has often arisen and flourished in times of confusion and chaos so that it can have the role of challenging by proposing a lifestyle based unambiguously on gospel values without compromise. The Church and the world need that witness. Even the poverty of our community may be seen to be a hidden grace. We are coming to the end of a generation, the generation that lived through the Council years. We are situated at that point of transition that I spoke of as the time of the desert, a place of paschal dying and rising in Christ to a new life that will be lived by another generation with the same ideals who will carry the torch forward in their own way.

The continuation of the charism of St Bruno, the charism of a community of men or women living a solitary contemplative life, corresponds to something so fundamental in human spiritual experience and in the identity of the Church of Christ that its continuation, to my mind, is assured. The cultural envelope and means of expression may change, but that is not important. We can go forward in hope, confidence and joy, bearing the face of Christ turned towards the Father, windows of the love of the Spirit of God and human beings. Like St Bruno, let us do so always with joyful countenance (*semper festo vultu*).

CALLED TO BE SAINTS

Feast of All Saints, 1 November 1994

The trouble is that we are called to be saints, not just good people, virtuous, wise, well-balanced, not doing harm to others. We are called to be holy as God is holy, to be perfect as our heavenly Father is perfect, merciful as he is merciful, loving as Christ loves us, that is totally, to the point of giving our life for our brothers and sisters.

This is surely a tall order. If we look at our own experience of life, if we look at ourselves and the people we know and have known, do we see many saints, do we see any? Would I be able to recognise a saint if I saw one? This is not at all certain. It would imply that I know exactly what makes a saint a saint. In an abstract way I could perhaps say something on that subject. I could say that a saint is someone who has responded fully to the gift of God communicating himself to a human person in the reality of his historical existence, this person thus becoming godly, begotten as a child of God, living and to live for all eternity from God's life. I could say that a saint is someone wholly animated and transformed by the Spirit of Christ, becoming like Christ in his or her heart and actions. I could say that a saint is someone utterly empty of self, given wholly in service of God and his or her neighbour. I could say that a saint is a person of profound faith, hope, love, goodness, humility, generosity, prayer, truthfulness. I would be right, of course, although I am then rather describing the effects of sanctity than touching on its core.

The essential of the saint, it seems to me, is the divine spark of grace in a saint's soul, that something of God's Spirit that is freely given and as freely received. This is what lifts a human life to a plane other than the realisation of a human project or ideal to something more sublime but also disconcerting. God ultimately is mystery, transcending all our categories and reasonable previsions and the saint, who lets God shine through, is equally mysterious and unpredictable. Touched by God, the saint is creative of what is new. How often in the history of the Church have the saints been the initiators of original ways of being Christ in the world. What an enormous variety there is in the styles of life and personal being they have manifested. The vitality of the Gospel of Christ is nowhere more clear as it responds to the needs of each epoch. In that respect the canonisation of some saints (there are many more uncanonised saints, perhaps the majority) can be falsely understood if it is regarded as limitative, that is, we must imitate them in exactly their way of living. We cannot all be like St Thérèse of Lisieux! Christ alone is to be imitated in the strict sense, and then, as it were, from within, under the guidance of his Spirit. The example of the saints encourages us to something of the same quality of commitment but embodied according to the particular grace of each one. Let us not be afraid to be original in this sense, as long as it is the expression of the originality of the Holy Spirit.

This, of course, is why we might not recognise a saint. He or she might not fit any one of our familiar models. We tend to see only the exterior discrepancies from what we expect in a saintly person and the inevitable limitations, that may have nothing to do with his or her liberty and hence sanctity. Perhaps we are surrounded by saints that we fail to recognise, just as Christ was not recognised in the poor and hungry and naked (Matthew 25: 31–46). It is not for us to judge. Let us receive and cherish Christ in each one of our brothers and sisters and, for our part, be faithful to the grace we have received. Then our voice will blend perfectly, without losing its original tone, with the voices of all the saints throughout all time, in all places, as we sing the praises of our God and Father in the melody of his Son and the breath of his Spirit. We will start to do that hopefully in the office we are about to celebrate. Happy feast!

IF GOD EXISTS

Receiving the Habit as Cloister Monk,
Feast of the Presentation of the Lord, 2 February 1995

If God exists, the taking of the Carthusian habit today has sense, is even rigorously coherent. If God does not exist, then you are a fool, the victim of a self-destroying illusion. Everything hangs on this one question, and will go on depending on it every day and night of the years that will be given to you to live. The contemplative life is not primarily a business of heroism. It is rather the common-sense ordering of our attitudes and acts according to the vision of things given to us by faith. Faith is the key, animated by the love of him who is the source and end of all that is, and sustained by the hope that awaits the fulfilment of his promise. If God exists, we must surely adore him in his majesty, obey him in his commands, receive his gift of life with gratitude and trust, love him in his goodness and his beauty, live in communion with him in so far as we are able, see and love all creatures, particularly our brothers and sisters, as he sees and loves them, up to the giving of our life for them in Christ, if this is asked of us. All this follows necessarily, if God exists.

The problem is that the act of faith reaches out beyond the limits of our rational mind and points towards a mystery it cannot circumscribe or control. Love of the Good seen in shadow and enigma alone can bear our mind on the wings of trust into direct contact with the reality of God as he is in himself. The ultimate guarantee of our faith must paradoxically be God alone. Our act of faith is his own light gifted to us and is its own truth. Light is light. It is a fact that faith becomes, not visions, but vision, the simplest and clearest of all. But it is also this leap in trust in God, and this aspect may be foremost at certain key moments.

You yourself have used the expression 'le saut de l'ange'. This refers to a dive from the high board into a swimming pool with arms outstretched until the very last second. Only, in this case, the diver cannot see for himself whether he is diving into water or on to a cement surface. People gathered around the pool tell him to jump, the pool is full of water – let us say that they represent the Church – while others, the non-believers, cry that the pool is empty and you will crash on to a cement floor. This illustrates well the place of the testimony of the Church in our faith, but the saints who have jumped do not come back to tell us how it was. Again, ultimately, with the whole Church, we must put our trust in the Word of God himself who invites us to take him at his word and enter into his kingdom and life, by adhering to Christ and following in his footsteps, through death to life eternal. Perhaps we of all people will experience the anguish of this act at certain moments, for we are suspended from an unique cord. Perhaps the essence of the contemplative life is to believe in God because he is God, to love him for his own sake, and to hope for nothing less than God himself, giving himself to each one of us in a total communion of life and love.

For you, of course, there is the added complication that the pool in question is situated in an English garden! The Carthusian ideal has always been seen by you clothed in the form of a certain natural setting: the glory of the mountains, the purity of snow, the silence of high spaces. The Lord in his providence has led you to pitch your tent in another setting, with a less obvious poetry. As in so many areas of your life, you are invited to relinquish an exterior reality in order to accede to a deeper spiritual reality. England, behind the more bland appearance, is indeed a spiritual desert in many ways and has desperate need of the witness of men of prayer to the reality of God. You show that you have the intuition of the value of witness of a life given totally and publicly consecrated to God by your devotion to a great English martyr, St Thomas More. His initial attraction to the Charterhouse took the final form of suffering physical death for his faith. Perhaps your initial and enduring call to the priesthood may find its concrete realisation in the offering of your whole life, day after day, body and soul, as what St Paul calls 'a living sacrifice, holy and acceptable to God, which is your spiritual worship' (Romans 12:1 RSV).

In today's feast, Simeon and Anna receive and acknowledge the Saviour in a little child. Each one of us must learn to discern the image of Christ engraved in the Child within us – the Child who, in his spontaneity and vulnerability yet dares to dream great dreams and to go forward towards their realisation in the joy of hope. That Child will not be crushed by a life dedicated to Christ for he is, in truth, 'Christ within you, the hope of glory' (Colossians 1:27). Believing in him who is, who was, and who will be, and putting on Christ Jesus, your Lord and Saviour, will you now, this day, set forth on this way?

'JOY AND WOE ARE WOVEN FINE . . .'

First Sunday of Lent, 1995

Let us imagine that this will be our last Lent. For one or other of us this could easily be the case. For all of us, it is at least a possibility. This space of forty days then will bring us into the presence of the Lord. Let us live this time in that spirit.

The Israelites were forty years in the desert of Sinai before entering the promised land. Moses stayed forty days on the mountain to receive the Law. Jesus was led by the Spirit into the desert to be tempted for forty days. In our turn we will be tempted. The desert is no bland, idyllic place, 'idle as a painted ship upon a painted ocean' (*The Ancient Mariner*). It is, on the contrary, vibrant with dense reality. A part of that reality are the divisions and conflicts within our hearts, the struggle between good and evil reflecting that which can be observed on the wider canvas of the contemporary world. The two are not separate. Our interior struggle derives in part from and has in return a hidden but profound effect on humanity's course. Let us never forget it. The eternal lot of someone may depend on your difficult fidelity.

Remember St Anthony. Going into a greater solitude, he was immediately confronted with all the demons he carried within him: lust, avarice, anger, vanity, rebellion, pride, despair. Sounds familiar, doesn't it? Young monks will sometimes take this as an indication that they are in the wrong place, when in fact it merely manifests their truth and the purification that needs to be done, if they are to follow Christ with all their heart. Even those who have already advanced some way on the road will discover deeper areas of opacity in themselves, hidden resistance to the total opening of the heart to God. This is something that occurs in the intimate solitude of each one. It is in prayer and stillness that the essential work is done, often beyond our conscious awareness. It is favoured by a fasting from the superficial and distracting that reflects a hunger for the essential, a mind that is nourished by silence, an entering into, a being taken up into the deep pulse of all that is, the inflowing creative will of God. When we are totally identified with God's willing of all reality in the mystery of his love, we will become, in him, source of being to all created reality, animated by God's own life, giving

[85]

back what we have received, even God to himself. This is the Easter we prepare for, the resurrection already at work in us in faith and hope.

Let me try to capture this hidden presence of life. There are two liturgical gestures that are highly significant: both occur during the Mass, and have the added interest of joining the solitary and the community aspects of our Carthusian life. The first is the gesture of the priest at the altar when he extends his arms in the form of a cross. In doing so, obviously, he figures Christ, but what struck me recently, precisely from the position of the priest, is that the two choirs as it were prolong, almost seem to be, his outstretched arms. There is, in truth, but one priest, one offering. The second sign occurs at the communion when we make a circle around the altar, that is around Christ. It is so visible. We are many in our solitude and yet we are one Christ, the perfect circle. There is a solidarity beyond and above all the things that seem to separate and oppose, a durability beyond the passing presence and role of each individual. We are and will be for ever one body of Christ. May this mystery of unity, love and peace be realised in each one of you and in our community more and more this Lent so that Easter may be the unveiling of that life which is already ours in Christ.

CHRIST LIVES IN US

Easter Sunday, 1995

The fact that Christ has risen from the dead means that death is not the tragic or senseless last word on our life. The gift of life we have been given and that we receive at every instant is bigger. It includes death within itself and goes on to an even higher realisation. This is what we celebrate at Easter and what determines our whole understanding of who and what we are. The Christian is essentially a person of hope and hence of joy. All will indeed be well, whatever the vicissitudes through which we must sometimes pass.

The risen Christ, his wounds transformed into sources of grace, has conquered in his humanity and he will do so in ours. For this is the direct consequence of the resurrection: the living Christ is present in us as an unquenchable source of life, knowing, loving, suffering at times, leading us by his Spirit into his passage from death to life, bringing us to the Father in eternal light. Each of us can say with Paul, 'It is no longer I who live, but Christ who lives in me; and the life I now live in the flesh I live by faith in the Son of God who loved me and gave himself for me' (Galatians 2:20 RSV).

Both as individuals and as the Church Christ lives in us and his Spirit guides us. The preoccupation of the coming General Chapter concerning the problems facing the Order because of the changing circumstances affecting our lifestyle is valid and must be addressed. But this can be done in an atmosphere of faith, without fear, and without the need to know and control everything so as to secure our future. We can open ourselves in trust and joy to the Spirit of him who lives in us and let ourselves be led along the mysterious paths of his grace, step by surprising step, leaving behind what is to be left behind in order to be free to receive the gift that Love's ingenuity will give in good time. I find the newness of the creative work of the Spirit an exhilarating prospect; what will he think of next! The superabundant mystery of God's vitality will always be ahead of us, as it were. In so many of the post-resurrection appearances Christ says to his disciples: 'Do not be afraid. I am with you, I am in you.' May he be more and more this Easter time the real source of our life, our courage and our joy.

FATHER OF THE POOR

Pentecost Sunday, 1995

It seems appropriate to reflect a little on the recent General Chapter as a spiritual event. The Holy Spirit was present and active in a perhaps more visible way than usual. There was a distinct vitality, a shift of wind, a deeper reading of the signs of the times. What then was the Spirit saying to the Carthusian Church? The message would seem to be:

1 to recall our fundamental charism as a realisation of the paschal emptying and new life in Christ;
2 unity: among ourselves and with the whole Church whose great concerns we should actually assume;
3 mission: not by word but by presence, in the 'third world', in particular. 'As the Father sent me, so do I send you' (John 20:21 REB).

We have come too much to think of ourselves as a prestigious and respected Order, a spiritual élite, lighting the way for the less elevated, buttressed in massive, immemorial stone buildings. In the emblem 'Stat Crux dum volvitur orbis', we have insisted above all on the *stat*, our solid stability in face of the changing world. We have often forgotten the paradoxical fact that it is the cross that so stands. Unless it is the expression of the paschal mystery of Christ, our continuing existence is but the immobility and persistence of organic matter and institutional habit.

Our charism is first of all to live the mystery of Christ's self-emptying, his kenosis, in loving faith in the Father, and to incarnate the new life-gift of the resurrection in the eternal newness of the Spirit. We are to do this in a special way, characterised by the predominance of God's Word received in prayer, solitude and silence, so as to let God communicate himself (as much as possible) in the Holy Trinity. From this point of view, we perceive our real personal and community poverties, not as aberrations to be got rid of by spending more money, but as the expression of our reality and our grace. Our poverty is the place of our riches. It is what is freely embraced in order to transform it in the glory of the Father. God is our past, God is our future and we find him in Christ in our present. He is not enclosed in our time. It is in constantly

[89]

beginning again, each day, each moment, in faith, love and hope that we are in his eternity. By willing at every instant the reality that he wills, we will God himself as he is and are most intimately united to him in trust and love.

In the General Chapter this recall of the spiritual theological source of our vocation led us to remember the humble nature of the historical beginnings of our Order. St Bruno gives us an example of a difficult, searching fidelity to an interior call to communion with God in silence and solitude. He left much to follow it and had to leave his first foundation and community in obedience to the Church's need. The first community of Carthusians also were a fragile group of men, living a precarious life in poor wooden cabins, soon to be destroyed in an avalanche. They called themselves the poor of Christ, *pauperes Christi*, and they were that in fact. The Carthusian Order came about when a number of communities, equally poor, striving towards the same ideal, came together freely and drew strength and continuity from their union expressed in the General Chapter and their submission to it. We need to find anew the spontaneous fraternal character of that union beyond the scaffolding of juridical prescriptions and centralisation that has grown, perhaps inevitably, with time. The Spirit is clearly at work in the slow transforming of the atmosphere and style of government.

More conscious of our real identity in Christ, and of our communion among ourselves, the General Chapter found itself more open to the invitation of the Spirit to listen to what the Church was asking of us. In spite of our perceived poverty, particularly in people, with a surge of faith and confidence the General Chapter became conscious of its missionary vocation, i.e., of its responsibility towards the Church and the world to be a beacon of the light of Christ by the very life we live. It had the courage to orient us towards the eventual implantation of the Carthusian life outside Europe, outside even those countries, such as America, still close to European culture. It is a momentous step and may have far-reaching consequences for our Order. Whatever the future holds, everybody was surprised by the quasi-unanimity of votes and the firm spirit of faith beyond all merely human prudence. We do not know where God is leading us and we do not need to know. That is just the point. It will be his work, not ours.

In different houses in various countries there is a stirring of life: many new members, remarkable providential events, in general a buoyancy of spirit. We too can see Christ's mystery in our poverty and the action of his Spirit in our faith that our strength and our hope is in the Lord, and that we must open our hearts more and more to be guided by the Spirit from within in prayer, detachment from all self-seeking, unbounded faith and trust, communion between us, and the peace and joy that will follow. If the Carthusians are the poor of Christ, the Holy Spirit is, as the liturgy says, *pater pauperum*: the Father of the poor. May we more and more live as sons of that Father.

THE GARDENER

Receiving the Habit as Donate Brother,
Feast of Sts Peter and Paul, 29 June 1995

When Mary Magdalen first saw the risen Christ, she supposed him to be a gardener (John 20:15). This is fitting, as God himself is described as a vinedresser in one of Christ's parables. To illustrate the step you are taking today and the way that lies before you, I will use two well-known gospels.

The first is that of the householder who hired labourers for his vineyard, at the first, third, sixth, ninth and, even, eleventh hour. I will not try to determine too precisely at what hour you see yourself but, let us say, it is at least in the afternoon. Whatever, the Lord has called you into his vineyard and you have responded, and, very visibly, you have got to work with much energy. In general, St Hugh's looks like it has had a giant hair-cut! It looks, thanks to you, cared for and tidy.

This expresses your enthusiasm, and mirrors a more interior work that must also be done. To grasp something of the dimensions of the spiritual work, I will turn to the parable of the vine in St John (15:1–11 RSV). I will only paraphrase the text, it is so rich and so meaningful. The vineyard, and the kingdom of God it figures, is not a place into which we enter, it is Christ, in whom we abide.

'I am the true vine, and my Father is the vinedresser.' A vinedresser who, beyond our own efforts and wisdom, acts himself and purifies our hearts. 'Every branch of mine that bears no fruit, he takes away, and every branch that does bear fruit he prunes that it may bear more fruit.' To prune is to cut off what does not bear fruit, not as we see it, but as God in his wisdom and demanding love sees it. One can easily imagine the panic of the vine that is stripped of parts of itself that seemed essential. Yet relinquish them we must.

We can do so because, our Lord reassures us, his living virtue is already active in us, in a hidden way. His work, at some level, is already realised. 'You are already made clean by the word which I have spoken to you', and which we have received in faith and trust. The transformation of our whole being will take time.

Our task is to dwell in Christ, so that his life may flow in us. 'Abide in me and I in you. As the branch cannot bear fruit by itself, unless it abides in the vine, neither can you unless you abide in me.' This is the principle we must never forget. All our efforts at recollection, meditation, vigilance, prayer, liturgy, service in obedience, aim at this one thing.

'I am the vine, you are the branches. He who abides in me and I in him, he it is that bears much fruit, for apart from me you can do nothing.' Let us never be found apart from Christ. Even our weaknesses and our sins need not separate us from him who is the source of healing and saving love. We need only and constantly to return to him in humility and faith, for he has come to call sinners and to save them.

If we live in Christ, our prayer, our intercession for all, without exclusion of any, will be received by the Father as the voice of Christ, and will be efficacious. 'If you abide in me, and my words abide in you, ask whatever you will, and it shall be done for you. By this my Father is glorified, that you bear much fruit, and so prove to be my disciples.'

And, in Christ, we are drawn into the prodigious exchange of love that is the Holy Trinity. 'As the Father has loved me, so have I loved you; abide in my love. If you keep my commandments, you will abide in my love, just as I have kept my Father's commandments and abide in his love.'

The sign of the reality of that love poured forth in our hearts and of a life guided by its precepts is joy, Christ's joy in our hearts: 'These things I have spoken to you that my joy may be in you, and that your joy may be full.'

Brother William, will you follow Christ in this way?

BEAUTY BOUND

Feast of St Bruno, 6 October 1995

As many of you are young Carthusians, it may be of interest to try to capture something of the essential inspiration of St Bruno. This will only be the few strokes of the artist's pencil that evoke some aspects of his subject. Each of you would do as well.

Entering the Charterhouse consists in a turning from something, or rather some things, and a turning towards something, some one thing. What we turn from is much less important than what we turn towards, even if we have great difficulty in describing or defining it. If we could do so, we would touch the kernel of Bruno's vocation, which is an obscure perception of the mystery of God, something of his transcendent beauty and a call to enter into it. It is a thing of light and wonder, like the rising of the sun which makes all the glittering man-made lights pale into insignificance and which, yet, is as common and natural as walking in the daylight.

It is, of course, a thing of the mind, or the mind-heart to be more exact, an interior reality that nevertheless changes our sensible perception. It introduces us into the vast world of faith, a world we shall never finish exploring in this life and in the next. From the outside, contemplative life seems boring and monotonous. From within, it is the opposite. The tiniest being, a ladybird or 'God's cow' (as it is called in this part of the country) for example, a faceted stone, a cheeky robin, is a source of simple joy and communion. Consciously, to be is such a marvellous experience! Had we but the courage of joy.

The three strokes I will use to evoke Bruno will be thanksgiving, sacrifice and adoration.

Thanksgiving, because all is gift, given, surprise, unearned, gracious generosity, love's considerate coming to us.

Sacrifice, because of love. To love is to go out of self, to give, to lose oneself in the gift. This implies a sometimes bloody tearing of the bonds of selfishness, fear, distrust, grasping, possessiveness, sin. Christ is the way and the truth of this paschal aspect of our human historical reality. Death is its moment of finality. The living of that finitude in time and in hope is the essence of asceticism in the Christian sense. It is the source of a great liberty, when freely embraced, and, in Christ, a source of healing and redemption for all.

Adoration, because God is God. Even the little that filters through the stained-glass windows of creation fills us with wonder before his beauty, with awestruck stillness and reverent joy. We are indeed so little, he so great, and yet by his goodness, communion is possible. Our earthen vessel can contain and reflect a heavenly fire. Perhaps the lucid consciousness of these two almost opposite realities in one being is the existential paradox of our type of life, its constant impossible balancing act.

In all simplicity then, let us today, like St Bruno, step boldly into the mystery of the world of faith and praise the triune God, Father, Son and Holy Spirit, as we are born into the plenitude of eternal life.

GOD'S WAITING

Feast of the Immaculate Conception of the Blessed
Virgin Mary, 8 December 1995

I will try to express the relation, dimly perceived, between two things: on the one hand, the incredible grandeur of the universe; on the other, the idea of waiting as characterising not only this liturgical time but humankind and God himself.

You may have read the article from *Time* showing the amazing pictures obtained by the Hubble Space Telescope. Situated in space, outside the distortions of the earth's atmosphere (a good example for the contemplative eye!), this telescope allows us to look deeper and more clearly into the immense space and time of the universe. We can see stars and galaxies being born on a scale that literally dwarfs our little world and galaxy. One cannot help being filled with awe and wonder before the immense power, splendour and beauty of God's creation and hence of God the creator. 'What indeed is man that you should care for him, O Lord?' (Psalm 8:4).

There is, however, another thought. This cosmic splendour was waiting to be discovered, we might say. Not in the sense that it existed before exactly as it does now, except that there was no spectator. No; before, it was a physical fact only. Now, something of its power of meaning has been recognised and acknowledged by a knowing mind, a mind that suffers the passion of its beauty, opens up to it and receives it as it is. In this meeting of the material reality and the spiritual mind, both exist in a new and fulfilled way, the spirit receives meaning and gives importance to the world.

But humankind is made in the image of God. Does this then tell us something about God? The cosmos waits for human understanding. Humans must wait to receive the power from the universe, suffer it, as it were, then acknowledge it with understanding and love. Humans are those who wait: it is our contemplative dimension and it is more fundamental than our activity on the world. Can we change the smallest of nature's laws? Can we cause the smallest spark in the immensity of the cosmos? No, but we can receive, understand and give it being in meaning and praise.

Is there a waiting in God? What can he be said to wait for? Not for the physical creation, evidently. And in so far as waiting implies something having importance for us, and thus love of and dependence on it, God can never be under any necessity to wait for anything. Pure act, infinite being, he needs nothing. He is impassible, cannot be controlled and manipulated. This is true and must never be lost sight of. Yet his power goes much further. He can choose to be dependent on his creature, in choosing to love him, to give himself into his hands in the person of Christ, to be dependent on human reception or rejection of him. He is not an impassive spectator; he 'suffers' (*passus*) humankind. He gives importance to humankind and so can be in the position of one who waits. We wait only for what counts for us.* One cannot be said to wait for a train that one does not wish to travel on. The terrible banality of so many lives comes from the fact that nothing really matters to them; there is nothing to hope or wait for. This is flat numb despair. God, who has given all, waits freely and without necessity, vulnerable and exposed, on our recognition and response of love. The Father is forever eagerly awaiting, hoping for the return of the prodigal son. And with what patience! On another plane, think of the huge cosmic time before eyes of recognition opened on the universe!

This is the extraordinary God that Christmas reveals to us: the paradoxical beauty that exists in the tension between the awesome cosmic immensity, that somehow, for me, figures the beginnings of redemption in the Immaculate Conception, and the utter vulnerability of the newborn infant, given, helpless, into the hands of its parents and the world, waiting, in hope, on what will be.

In this is love, in this is God, that God first loved us and gave himself up for us.

---

* Raskolnikov discovers his love for Sonia when he finds himself *waiting* for her, in Dostoevsky's *Crime and Punishment*.

I LIKE LENT

First Sunday of Lent, 1996

Dean Swift, the author of *Gulliver's Travels*, wrote that he hated Lent. 'I hate different diets and furmity and butter [for us, margarine], and herb porridge; and sour devout faces of people who only put on religion for seven weeks.'

On the contrary, I like Lent. I like the long mornings, the quality of a silence that waits with baited breath. I like the wise path traced out for us by the Word of God in all its power under the pedagogy of the Church. I like the revisiting of essential things, the performing of ancient rites that initiate us into the ultimate secrets of life and death, the ever new path trodden with Christ.

There are, of course, physical deprivations, but they are not crippling. There may be conflict between the forces of good and evil in ourselves, for the desert is the place of the weighing of hearts. All to the good. On the other hand, there is a movement welling up from the earth like the sap in the trees, an awakening from the sleep of winter. The wind is cold, the rain insistent, the branches bare, yet spring is not far off. A timid shoot pushes through the earth, a cock finch bursts into sudden song before a moment of warm sunlight, herald of hope to a surprised audience. A gentle light filters through the doors of days that open wider and wider. That is why this season was called 'Lent', a word which means 'spring', a time when the days are lengthening, a time of resurrection and new life springing from the darkness of death.

Dust we are and to dust we shall return, but this is not the end of our human journey. Out of the ashes will rise a new life of another order. Asceticism is but a training and a preparation for a greater quality of life, a voluntary going beyond the limits of our earth-bound appetites in order to set free other capacities for life, ultimately a passage in Christ to the Life beyond death. I wish you all an abundance of that life and that joy that no one will take from you for ever.

THE FESTIVAL OF LIGHT

Easter Sunday, 1996

Early this morning in the narthex before the door of the church we lit a candle in the dark. From that candle each of us symbolically took light, and we followed that candle into the church and we set it there in a place of honour.

What could symbolise better the festival of light that is Easter, light shining in the darkness?

First there was the darkness, outside, without light, the place of primal fears and uncomprehending suffering, of evil and sin; the powers of darkness are evil. Yet darkness represents also the potentiality of light, the word itself implies its absence, therefore its reality and its possibility. Our night prayer is enveloped in darkness, but another darkness, one of waiting in hope, of prayer in faith. There is a blessed night just as there is a damned one. The difference lies in the act of trusting faith that sees without seeing.

Then, still outside, fire springs up where there was none, created as it were from the stuff of the universe (actually, not being God, Bogdan did have to employ a created intermediary, namely a match!). The candle is lit. The candle represents Christ, our Saviour, come to dispel our darkness with the flame of his risen life. Just one centre of light and all is changed. The candle is marked with the insignia of his glory: the alpha and the omega: he is the source and end of all creation; the cross, the means of his total redemptive giving of himself for love of us all. Sometimes five grains of incense are added: the five wounds through which his love was poured out on us, fragrance of adoration. Simply, 'Christ our light'.

We followed Christ into the church, into the place of the divine majesty, filled now, not with darkness, but with the light of his purifying mercy. At the door of the church the flame was communicated to each one from that of Christ. Easter is the great celebration of the sacrament of baptism and confirmation by which we are engrafted into Christ and share in his risen life. Children of the light, we followed Christ into the Father's house, the flame without having become Spirit within. And there we reflected on the history of humankind's journey and God's mercy, and we sang the praises of our Lord and God and gave him thanks. Our joy no one will take from us. The candle will be there all during the Paschal time to remind us. The love we hold and that holds us – may it consume silently and gently the substance of our being in time, so that we may one day, beyond days, become pure flame in Christ. This I wish for you all, this blessed Easter.

CHRIST IS OUR HOMELAND

First Profession of a Cloister Monk,
Feast of the Ascension of the Lord, 1996

'Greater love has no man than this,
that a man lay down his life for his friends.'
(John 15:13 RSV)

The feast of the Ascension celebrates the passage of the Risen Christ from being present in the world in the mysterious yet visible and tangible way, to a more hidden, real sacramental mode of presence. There is a going away, a being lifted up out of sight to the right hand of the Father, i.e., into the transcendent sphere of the divine nature. The disciples are bereft. Their only recourse is to come together along with Mary, and give themselves to prayer and to waiting; to waiting for the gift of the Holy Spirit that Christ has promised. The Spirit does come, visible at Pentecost, more interiorly every time a heart opens itself to God. As he is the Spirit of the Son and of the Father, he realises a new mode of presence of Christ within hearts, animating, guiding, loving, praying, sustaining, making us children of God, one Body of Christ. It is indeed to our advantage that Christ should go away.

This archetypal event of Christ's Ascension has to be realised in the life of each one of us who are baptised into Christ if we are to attain to the fullness of the stature of Christ. We too have to ascend to the Father in Christ. St Paul says that we already have ascended, in so far as we are included by faith in Christ. He draws the logical conclusion: 'If then you have been raised with Christ, seek the things that are above, where Christ is, seated at the right hand of God. Set your minds on things that are above, not on things that are on earth' (Colossians 3:1–2 RSV). Christ is our homeland, elsewhere we are strangers.

This call to live as children of God, to live at the level of what we are in Christ and not just as, however rational, animals: this call is clear and mandatory. As monks, we have and do try to respond to it. However, this is not an invitation to live as pure spirits. This is the paradox of Ascension. Christ has ascended into heaven and yet Christ will be with us on earth till the end of time. In Christ, we too share his risen life and we too live on earth, or rather, Christ lives in and through us in space and time.

Christ continues to be present on earth in the Church through the gift of the Spirit, through his Word and the sacraments of his active presence. So our life on earth is transformed into Christ-life, by the Spirit, the Word and the sacraments. All this is most strongly seen in the sacrifice of the Mass, which is the point of assumption of our whole human reality, flesh, heart and spirit, into the incandescent crucible of Christ's love for us and the Father, rendered sacramentally present.

Our human life is eucharistic, becoming thanksgiving and adoration by the transforming power of loving sacrifice. By allowing our whole human reality to be taken up into the love of Christ, we participate in his redemptive mission towards our brothers and sisters. As Christ assumed a whole and complete humanity, so too must we be drawn up into his sacrificial love. The whole of our humanity, its grandeur and its baseness, its gifts and its sins (Christ wants our sins too!), its heroism and its cowardice, its capacity to love and share, and its grasping egoism. It is only from within our flawed humanity, in the communion of saints and in that of sinners, that healing, forgiving grace can flow. The moments of pain, hurt and shame in solitude, in Christ, can be moments of redemptive communion, priestly time. This is the heart of monastic profession. 'Greater love has no man than this, that a man lay down his life for his friends' (John 15:13 RSV). Our nature may shrink from this and rebel, yet we know there lies our peace. 'Peace I leave you. My peace I give unto you' (John 14:27). Do not fear, it is not a question of our own strength but of that of God, testifying to his grace in our weakness. For 'I will be with you all days, even to the end of time' (Matthew 28:20).

THE SEARCH FOR THE ETERNAL GOOD

Feast of St Bruno, 6 October 1996

The prayers of the Office for today's feast insist on fidelity to our vocation and perseverance in it. St Bruno is, of course, a model that can help us to focus on the essential of our life and to continue with sureness in this way.

Happily, Bruno himself describes the nature of his calling in his letter to Raoul le Verd. The three friends, Bruno, Raoul and Foulcroie le Borgne were conversing in the garden of the house of Adam. 'We spoke for some time of the false attractions and passing riches of this world, and of the joys of eternal glory. Then burning with love of God, we promised, we made a vow to quit soon the fugitive shadows of the world and to receive the monastic habit, in order to give ourselves to the search for the eternal good.'

There were three who felt drawn by God to this, but only one fulfilled it. All the subsequent history of Bruno is the realisation of this promise to turn his face resolutely towards God and eternal things and away from the vanity and ambitions of this ephemeral world. The hidden life he embraced, the founding of the Chartreuse, the return to this form of life in Calabria after the episode of his being called to the aid of the Pope in Rome, his perseverance until death in his chosen way – all this was the concrete expression of his seeking after and adhering to God, his resting in Christ. The Customs of the Carthusian life, and subsequently our Statutes, are meant to order every aspect of a life that has this as its basic direction and goal.

We ourselves have to come back constantly to this original inspiration, inspired indeed by the Holy Spirit in our founder. This is our charism in the Church, the function we are asked to fulfil, that of a hidden heart that beats within and animates all the members in the degree of our charity and faith.

Perseverance is not just a question of maintaining a past engagement. Our liberty is realised in time. Day by day, year by year, whatever the vicissitudes and events we live through in God's providence, we have to renew, realign, if necessary reassume our turning towards God, espouse the harmony of the essential order of things by creatively willing God's eternal willing. New-born in Christ, each day we direct our steps in his and enter into the mystery of his quietness. Our time is paschal time, our life is new life hidden with Christ in God, our vocation to explore the depths of God's silence and participate in his Love.

May this feast of St Bruno be a new beginning, constantly chosen and reaffirmed, a beginning without end.

TO THE UNKNOWN SAINTS

Feast of All Saints, 1 November 1996

I would like to dedicate these few reflections to the unknown saints that people the kingdom of heaven. They will be in the vast majority. The saints the Church has identified and confirmed are but a tiny number in comparison with the uncounted millions, rather billions, who will find their home in heaven.

I find it wonderful that the Church sets aside a day in which to celebrate this motley throng of 'ordinary' saints, bringing together in one great sweep this huge diversity of human beings, each one reflecting some aspect of Christ's face. It will surely be one of the great joys of paradise, if hopefully we get there ourselves, to contemplate the trans-figured faces of so many unlikely, unexpected, and totally ordinary people. I think of the last judgement not as of a stern judge passing out sentences but as of a jubilant Father revealing to all the hidden riches of his joyful children. Embedded in their everyday, taken-for-granted, down-to-earth persons is a core of Christlike divinity. We shall, I think, often laugh with amazement at God's humour. The last will indeed be first.

To illustrate, my uncle Tom comes to mind. He was a smallish stocky black-haired man. Intelligent and well read though without much formal education, he started earning his living at fourteen. He did many things. At one time he was a professional golfer, then in later years a butcher. He went to Mass on Sundays, his faith was a given, he tried to be not 'good' but fair and honest to others. He could always be counted upon to help anyone in need. He lived an ordinary life, liked a pint of Guinness, a game of cards and a discussion. He could talk to any man. With what he called 'sweat-money', he paid for the bus that took my family to my ordination to the priesthood. On that occasion, in his simple reverence for the priest I now was, he confided to me that he had never done deliberate harm to anyone and that he was sure that God would receive him into heaven because he had never failed to say a Hail Mary every day of his life. He died soon after. One day, I do hope to find him and all the multitude of his like and friends in Christ. Please God, on that day, we shall meet again and really know, love and celebrate all our unknown brothers and sisters in Christ. May today be a small beginning of that celebration.

A COMING TO LIFE

First Profession of a Cloister Monk,
Christmas Day, 25 December 1996

We are surrounded by images of life and of death. They seem so close, so somehow alike. There is the babe in the crib, celebrating God's unlikely presence in the heart of our humanity. That celebration can be gay and imaginative, to judge from the display at the door of the chapterhouse! Then there is the gallant Brother Christopher coming to the end of his journey, perhaps. In his dependence and level of basic existence he resembles more and more the new-born infant. And there is Thomas, somewhere between the two, taking a brave step in the following of Christ today, a step that is, at once, a dying and a coming to life. Birth implies a leaving of the mother's womb in order to attain to separate existence.

It is a dying to ego-self, not without pain and fear, that profession operates. In so far as you can, you will ratify the grace of baptism by putting on Christ in a new and more radical way. You give yourself to him with all your poverty in trust and love. What his grace has begun it will finish. The love of God purifies and fulfils beyond all we can understand or even desire. But it is hard to let go of the control of our lives, our faith is often weak. Walking on water can be frightening!

Again the image of death touches that of life. For Christ says 'Unless you become as little children, you shall not enter the kingdom of God' (Matthew 18:3). We must accept to be born again of the Spirit to a life that transcends the limits of our earthly life, to a personhood as sons of the eternal Father. As the infant in the natural order does not arrive fully made, so the son of God that you would be does not arrive in one act. He is given in germ and in capacity, and his potentialities must be developed and grow to maturity.

The essential is first to believe in the love God has for you and receive in trust and confidence the immense personal gift he makes you in calling you by your name, in calling you to himself. Because his grace would raise us above ourselves, we sometimes would prefer him to choose someone else and leave us in peace!

That would be a peace of lack of true personhood that assumes its isolation and so renders personality and real communion impossible. Beyond self-pity and revolt lies self-transcendence. So you must accept your part of the birth-pangs in Christ and follow him in his mysterious yet willing poverty and renunciation to the glory of the totally undreamed of newness of eternal life.

The document of your profession will be put on the altar (a document greatly adorned!). Profession is a eucharistic act, one of thanksgiving, adoration, self-offering and communion with Christ and the Church. The bread and wine that will be transformed into Christ are the days and years of your life, the tears and joys of your humanity, the defeats and victories of your battle towards personal liberty, the unhealed pain that opens your heart to the Lord and your brothers and sisters, the wounds of the Passion that the risen Christ still bears, the solitude that can become communion, the profound joy of being that needs only your simple yes to the mysterious wisdom and love of God's willing here and now.

On this day, may Mary be a mother to you, the Church your family, and may Christ be born in your heart.

THE INVISIBLE MAN

Feast of The Body and Blood of the Lord, 1997

Nudus, nudum Christum sequere.
Naked, to follow the naked Christ.

Patrick wakes up to find he has become invisible. He looks at his watch. He sees the watch, he reads the hour, but his wrist he does not see. Frightened, he jumps out of bed. His pyjamas stand upright but there is no one in them. All at once, he understands that he has become really invisible: he has separated himself from all that rendered him visible to himself and to others. If he does not find another form of presence to himself, he will disappear altogether. He sets off in quest of himself.

At first, it is amusing. He sees people who cannot see him. He sees much good but also much evil. He sees people true to life. Then he hears what they say of him – even his friends (and this is not pleasant). Eventually, he begins to feel very isolated, alone, misunderstood. Then he discovers that by using make-up and clothes he can be seen by others. He clothes himself, with satisfaction.

Thereupon, he makes a terrible discovery. The others also are invisible, but they do not know it! It is not real persons who speak to each other but personas constituted by make-up and clothes. Basically, there are only four or five styles of clothes – like four or five uniforms. Those wearing a blue uniform range themselves against those wearing red. Not only are individuals reduced to being ciphers of a common type, but they are divided into cliques, each clique divided from and fighting the others. Finally, in their true identity, they are invisible, unknown and terribly alone.

What is to be done? Patrick has a blinding intuition – like a child seeing the sun rising in the morning for the first time. Naked, he will follow the naked Christ. Throwing off his uniform, washing all the make-up from his face, he stands naked. He accepts the solitude of the mystery of his being and his total poverty.

He enters a church where Mass is being said. For the first time he understands and lets himself be taken up into the movement of Christ's sacrifice, this total gift to the Father for the love of humankind, where he receives everything. The priest, a truly spiritual man, with the eyes of faith and hope, sees him in his invisibility. When Patrick eats the Body of Christ, his own body takes on again its true substantiality. He is there, visible, but different. He 'sees', in his turn, the others around him in their Christic bodies, and for the very first time, he can communicate with them – person to person. And in this communion – in loving his brothers – he discovers who he is. He is saved. He is no longer alone.

INDWELLING LOVE

Feast of the Most Holy Trinity, 1997

Today, we celebrate, not some aspect of the revelation, not some saint, but God himself in his innermost being. Hence the importance of the feast. Even though it dates only from the mid-fourteenth century, the Sundays following it used to be named with relation to it: 1st, 2nd, etc. Sunday after Trinity.

The explicit celebration of the Holy Trinity is fundamental to the knowledge we have of God and of ourselves. It is easy to slip into an idea of God derived from the abstract reasoning of Platonism, combined with a monarchical imperialism. The inscrutable God of predestinarian Calvinism, the implacable God of Jansenism, and the distant God of the eighteenth-century Deism, have alike imprinted a pattern on the Western understanding of God, which had little place for God as Trinity. It is this God that not only Marx, Freud and Nietzsche rejected, but also a sincere modern humanism. This negative image of God is often at the root of conflict with or revolts towards God to be found in the heart of many believers.

As if by reaction from such a remote and arbitrary God, in modern times the immanence of God has been stressed to the point that God seems often to be so telescoped into the world as to be identified with it. There is nothing more. As Coleridge put it, 'Pantheism is but a painted atheism – and the doctrine of the Trinity the only sure and certain bulwark against it.' Why? Because God as Trinity is a God of grace, the Lord and Giver of life, a God who saves.

And as our God is, so is our understanding of ourselves. There is here a circular influence. Human projections inevitably shape our image of God, but conversely our image of God shapes our understanding of what it means to be human. All too often the person is identified with the individual with adverse consequence. Persons are related by definition, individuals are not. Persons experience solitude, individuals isolation. Atomised individualism – me, me – and an equally destructive collectivism – we, we – have characterised much Western thought and political life in recent centuries. Both can be seen as flowing from a distorted doctrine of God, what has been called the pathology of Western Christianity, a failure to take Trinitarian theology seriously.

The heart of the doctrine of God is the conviction that God is a communion of persons. The Greek Fathers, in particular the fourth-century Cappadocians, spoke of that communion as *perichoresis*, a divine circulation of mutually indwelling love. This is God as he revealed himself in the person of Jesus Christ, this is how we must conceive of him as he is known through his self-giving and transforming love.

The Trinity is what we mean when we say that God is Love. That communion of Love is the key to our human identity as those made in the image of God. We come from each other in order to live for each other. And that is true socially as well as personally.

The feast of the Holy Trinity invites us to discover our true identity as persons in relationship, made in the image of the God of love, distinct from one another yet receiving and giving all of ourselves one to the other. We need to listen to what Gerard Manley Hopkins called 'the crying of those three, the Immortals of the Eternal Ring, utterer, uttered, uttering'. God, who is the source and goal of our being, is grace and communion. 'It is the glory of His high estate. He is an act that doth communicate' (Traherne). And he that dwells in love, dwells in God, and God in him (cf. 1 John 4:16). Let us, today, celebrate with joy and simplicity the fountain of love and life that God is.

THE SECRET OF SOLITUDE

Feast of St Bruno, 6 October 1997

Solitude is one of the ultimate questions for every human being. Finally, are we alone, coming into and leaving life, unknowing and unknown, unloving and unloved? This question is linked to that of purpose: Is there a sense to our existence, a purpose and value?

Solitude, as an important dimension of a lifestyle such as ours, expresses paradoxically the will to go beyond solitude as aloneness and absence of meaning.

It is striking how preoccupied modern culture is with solitude. The more information is communicated, the bigger and quicker the access to what is happening all over the world, the more are people crushed beneath the perception of themselves as insignificant and alone. The universe is unfolded before us in all its splendour. Instead of adoration, this can cause despair.

In the Middle Ages, people reached out beyond themselves into the world of more or less apocalyptic religious speculation – and a second millennium is upon us – or into the cultural world of imaginative art such as that of Dante. Nowadays, the same need to reach out beyond is expresses more visually in the somewhat crude but innovative efforts of books and films to portray a world beyond our own, beings from other planets and even the reality of cosmic good and evil. Are we alone? Do we matter?

The solitary must first inhabit his solitude. It is there he can enter into his deepest self and find such answers as he may find. He will soon experience the extreme difficulty of seizing the unseizable, of knowing the inexpressible, of reaching out beyond the parameters of scientific knowledge, hopefully, partially, to another level of being, to a reality beyond all shapes and forms, the real what and finally who that is Being in and through itself.

Whatever experience he has will always be subject to another interpretation: illusion, hallucination, subconscious imaginary projection of fear and desire, incapacity to live in the stark world of absurdity.

Whatever explanation he gives, whatever words he proffers will never prove anything to those who do not share this experience. He will never have absolute proof of the rightness of his experience either for himself or for others. This does not exclude certitude.

His eyes are the eyes of faith: faith in a Reality that has taken the initiative to communicate with us. We are not alone. Our lives are not without purpose. We are willed to be by an intelligent love, called by name to be persons, known and knowing, loved and loving, whose deepest reality will never disappear. The trace of his presence draw us towards him (for personal he is, and must be, if we are persons). We cannot but be drawn, if we but open our eyes and listen to our hearts.

He speaks to us with the words of our human experience. He assumes in Christ a human face, in order to introduce us into his being and life. Nevertheless, we are modelled of clay. It is so hard for us, not for an hour, or a month, or a year, but for a whole lifetime with its tasks and seasons, to hold ourselves in his serenity. The flesh, the affectivity, the mind often clamour a food more congenial to them. Our fragile sense of self needs to be bolstered and expressed in activity, affirmation and achievement. We may try to escape too much beauty by deliberately disrupting the harmony. We deform reality by our neurotic needs, or flee it altogether in psychotic denial. Sometimes we sin in order to keep God at a safe distance.

But there is nowhere to hide. Christ has walked all our paths, even that of death. He comes to us in his innocence, even in our sin. He can cure our will not to be cured. His love will not be denied. Ultimately, we are not alone. We know it, whatever our words say. Hopefully, in the end, we will yield to the light of truth, accept to be loved and to love totally. Our silence will be the peace of fulfilment and the joy of adoration.

I think this is what St Bruno meant by his oft-repeated 'O Bonitas'.

THE ORDINARY IS DIVINE

Perpetual Donation of a Brother,
Feast of the Birthday of St John the Baptist, 24 June 1998

There must be a hidden symbolism in the fact of your making donation on the feast of a saint who is said to have gone about eating locusts, which the dictionary defines as 'African or Asian grasshoppers migrating in swarms and consuming all vegetation of districts'. Tastes are not to be argued with. However, John the Baptist was also known as a man who chose to lead a hidden life.

In every community there are and there must be quiet presences that make things work but are rarely adverted to. While the rest of us are still asleep around 4 or 5 in the morning a ghostly figure pushes the cart around the cloister gathering the gamelles (food-boxes) from the previous evening. This is particularly impressive in winter when the scene is lit by a swinging electric lantern. We wake up to find the work already done.

Did someone say that the ordinary and the useful are divine? If not, someone should have, at least in the same sense that the bread of the Eucharist becomes and is the Body of Christ by virtue of the consecration of the Holy Spirit. The useful and the ordinary, the ordinary useful is divine in so far as it is animated by the charity of service of God and your brothers. Every simple act becomes an act of love. It becomes a properly religious act, an act of worship, in so far as it is offered to God in intention.

By making perpetual donation you are now passing to a more radical gift of self. As St Thomas puts it, you offer no longer only the fruits, individual acts of virtue, but also the tree itself, the person, the source of all your future acts which are thus consecrated to God. The word *donation* says it well. It is derived from the Latin *donum* or *donare*, 'gift' and 'to give'. By donation you give yourself totally to God in so far as your liberty can impose its will on the future. By perpetual donation, you give yourself to God in an irrevocable way, reaching out in intention and in hope unto the eternity inhabited by God.

It is a unique opportunity to match the gratuity of love that God is and that is manifested in the gift of Christ to us, to respond to him in the only language that is really worthy of him. It brings you near to, like to Christ whose very essence is this gift from and total gift to the Father. Each day you can bring the offering of your daily service and join it to the bread and wine to be consecrated by the Spirit, knowing that it is already accepted by the Father. The fatigue and occasional sufferings of each day and of a tired body or mind can be associated with the sufferings of Christ and become a source of redemptive grace for fellow human beings that you may never know. The joy, fraternal charity, simplicity and beauty that will be present each day, if you but stop to see them, will also be poured into Christ's chalice and be a source of interior joy for many unknown. Your offering will be hidden in ordinariness and will be the more universal and fruitful for that. I will make a pun on your current task of keeper of the door but I, and all of us, can pray that at the end, in your turn, you will hopefully hear the Lord reply to your knock at heaven's door: 'Well done, good and faithful servant. You have been faithful over a little, I will set you over much; enter into the joy of your master' (Matthew 25:21 RSV).